The Ultimate Guide to Dark Psychology

Master The Art of Covert Manipulation, Gaslighting, and Psychological Warfare for Self-Protection

Strategic Minds Media

Table of Contents

Trigger warning: This book contains discussions and examples of dark psychology tactics, manipulation techniques, and gaslighting behavior that may be distressing or triggering for some readers. Topics include emotional abuse, manipulation, control tactics, and psychological harm. Reader discretion is advised. If you find yourself experiencing distress or discomfort while reading, please prioritize your mental well-being and consider seeking support or taking a break.

Introduction

Have you ever felt like you're living life on someone else's terms? Like you're merely a pawn in a game where others hold all the control? It's a disconcerting feeling, isn't it? You might find yourself nodding along, recognizing the nagging sense that something is amiss. That's where you are now, seeking answers, wanting empowerment, striving for control.

You're not alone. Many of us have walked that same path, feeling the weight of manipulation, gaslighting, and the subtle erosion of our autonomy. But here's the thing: You have the power to reclaim control. You have the power to understand, to defend, and to thrive. That's why you're here, isn't it?

Perhaps it was a moment of clarity, a realization that you needed to break free from the chains of manipulation. Or maybe it was a series of events, each one chipping away at your resolve until you finally said, "Enough." Whatever brought you here, understand this: You are seeking improvement. You are seeking to *ameliorate* your life—to make it better, stronger, and more resilient.

So, what can you expect from this book? Let me lay it out for you. By diving into these pages, you're getting shortcuts to understanding dark psychology and holistic strategies to recognize manipulation—and to defend yourself against it. It's all laid out in the A.M.E.L.I.O.R.A.T.E. framework:

- **Accessing dark psychology:** Gain a comprehensive understanding of what dark psychology is, its origins, and its evolution.

- **Manipulation—core concepts in psychology:** Equip yourself with fundamental knowledge about manipulation, empowering you to navigate its complexities.

- **Exploring the techniques road map:** Delve into the tactics and strategies used in psychological manipulation, arming yourself with insight.

- **Leading covert techniques in dark psychology:** Uncover covert tactics and learn how to wield them ethically and effectively.

- **Introducing self-protection:** Learn practical tactics and tips for safeguarding yourself against manipulation.

- **Overtures of gaslighting—a silent weapon:** Understand gaslighting inside out—its signs, its impact, and how to combat it.

- **Reframing your tool kit for psychological warfare:** Harness every tool you need for psychological resilience and ethical self-defense.

- **Accessing resilience post-manipulation:** Discover how to bounce back from manipulation, rebuilding yourself with resilience and positivity.

- **The ethical route:** Learn to balance manipulation with ethics, crafting strategies that empower without harming.

- **Exploring neurolinguistic programming (NLP):** Dive into the realm of NLP and its intersection with dark psychology, gaining valuable insights and strategies.

Imagine a life where you move through the world with confidence, where you can discern the subtle maneuvers of manipulation and respond with clarity and strength. Picture yourself in thriving relationships, free from the shackles of gaslighting and coercion. This isn't just a dream; it's within your reach.

The goal of this book is to tackle issues faced by many of us under the veil of manipulation and gaslighting:

- **Desire for empowerment:**

    o You're craving something that can change the game, something that puts you in the driver's seat of your own life.

    o This book guides you toward understanding the principles of psychology for self-defense and the ethical wielding of power, fostering confidence and assertiveness.

- **Vulnerability to manipulation:**

    o Whether it's in your professional endeavors or your personal relationships, you feel like your control is limited.

    o This book equips you with knowledge and strategies to recognize manipulation in its myriad forms and reclaim your autonomy.

- **Lack of self-awareness:**

    o Many of us stumble in the dark, unaware of our own thoughts, emotions, and vulnerabilities.

    o Discover tools within these pages to shine a light on the darkest corners of your psyche, fortifying your psychological defenses against manipulation.

- **Strained relationships:**

  - Gaslighting, manipulation, and emotional turmoil characterize your relationships, leaving you yearning for connection and trust.

  - This book serves as your road map to navigate human interaction with grace and resilience, cultivating relationships that nourish rather than drain your spirit.

It is time to demystify dark psychology. It's not about embracing some sinister force; it's about grasping the mechanisms at play in human interaction. Prior to gaining this knowledge, achieving empowerment over your life may have seemed out of reach. But now, armed with these techniques and strategies, you're ready to take control of your life.

Feel it in your bones: This is the right book for you. It's the tool you've been searching for, the road map to reclaiming your autonomy and forging a path to a brighter, more empowered future. So, are you ready to start this transformative quest? Your empowerment awaits.

Chapter 1:

Accessing Dark Psychology

In the realm of dark psychology, deception is the language of power. –Sun Tzu

You are at the gateway of understanding dark psychology and the insidious art of gaslighting. In this chapter, we start down a path to unravel the intricacies of the human mind's darkest corners, shedding light on the manipulative tactics employed by those who seek to control and dominate.

Dark psychology is not merely a concept; it's a place where manipulation reigns supreme. But fear not, for knowledge is power, and understanding the intricacies of dark psychology is the first step toward safeguarding yourself from its grasp.

We'll look deep into the origins of dark psychology, tracing its evolution through history and exploring how it has morphed and adapted to modern society. By understanding its roots, you'll gain valuable insights into the motives behind manipulative behavior, equipping you with the tools to recognize and resist it.

Armed with this knowledge, you'll emerge from this chapter with a firm understanding of dark psychology's background, poised to navigate the murky waters of manipulation with clarity and confidence. It's time to take control of your own narrative and reclaim your power from those who seek to exploit it.

Defining Dark Psychology

Dark psychology delves into the intricate workings of human behavior, especially in the realm of manipulation and persuasion. It's not just a study; it's a spotlight on the darker shades of our nature and how they're wielded to influence others.

Picture it as a spectrum. On one end lies positive psychology, focusing on growth, resilience, and well-being. Dark psychology, however, occupies the other end, dealing with themes like control, deception, and coercion.

Positive psychology is the study of well-being and happiness in people. It focuses on positive feelings, strengths, and good qualities to help people function better and be stronger. The goal is to understand and encourage positive emotions like joy, gratitude, and love, and to improve personal skills like being resilient, hopeful, and kind. Positive psychology offers a way to deal with the negative aspects of psychology, providing methods to handle being manipulated, building strength, and looking after oneself.

But hold up—it's not all doom and gloom. Just like a knife can cut bread or stab, dark psychology's tools can be employed for either good or nefarious purposes.

The crux lies in the intent behind their use. Persuasion, for instance, seeks to sway opinions through logic and reason, and is a tool wielded by both the saintly and the sly. On the flip side, manipulation resorts to coercion and force, aiming not to convince but to control. The difference? Intent.

Now, let's zoom into one of the darkest corners: gaslighting. It's a diabolical form of manipulation where the victim's reality is warped until they doubt their own sanity. Imagine being told the sky isn't blue until you start believing it. It's insidious because it isolates, leaving victims feeling like solitary voyagers in a sea of doubt.

Another tactic in this dark arsenal is negation, a subtle yet devastating technique. It's like chipping away at someone's confidence, bit by bit, until they're but a shell of their former self. Through constant criticism and disapproval, the manipulator breeds insecurity, making their target more pliable to their whims.

Knowledge is your shield, and awareness, your armor. Understanding the basics of dark psychology isn't just about defense; it's about reclaiming power. By recognizing these tactics, you can thwart attempts at control and even harness this knowledge to fortify your resilience and improve your life.

How Has Dark Psychology Changed Over Time?

Dark psychology isn't a new phenomenon—it's been lurking in human interactions for centuries. Back in ancient times, people wielded hypnosis, suggestion, and superstition to control others. Fast forward to today, and the game has evolved. Now, dark psychology techniques aren't just tools for individuals—they're shaping entire societies.

Dark psychology isn't just about messing with your mind on a personal level. It's infiltrated our media, politics, and public discourse. Propaganda, fake news, misinformation—these aren't just buzzwords; they're weapons in the arsenal of those looking to control narratives and sway opinions.

So, what's the fallout? Brace yourself, because it's heavy. Dark psychology isn't just playing mind games—it's tearing at the fabric of society. Picture polarization skyrocketing, divisions deepening, and conflicts escalating. Trust in institutions? Shot. Democratic values? Under siege.

So, what can you do? Find your power in knowledge. Understanding how dark psychology operates gives you an edge that allows you to be no longer a pawn, but a player. Armed with awareness, you can move through these murky waters with clarity and purpose.

Early Psychological Research on Dark Psychology

Early research in this field laid the groundwork for recognizing and addressing manipulative tactics, including gaslighting.

Stanley Milgram's Obedience Experiment

One notable study that paved the way for understanding manipulation was Stanley Milgram's obedience experiment, conducted in the 1960s. Milgram's work demonstrated how individuals could be easily influenced to commit morally questionable acts under the guise of authority (Main, 2023).

In this experiment, participants were in a room, faced with a choice: to administer pain or defy authority. Three people took part in the scenario: the experimenter, the learner, and the teacher. The learner was actually working with the experimenter, and the teacher was the real participant.

The teacher was told to give electric shocks to the learner whenever the learner answered a question incorrectly. These shocks began at a low level and got stronger with each wrong answer. Keep in mind that the learner was not actually being shocked, but they acted as if they were in pain and begged the teacher to end it. Regardless, the experimenter told the teacher to keep shocking the learner.

What unfolded was shocking, quite literally. Despite the learner's pleas, the majority of participants pressed on, increasing the voltage to dangerous levels. This wasn't mere obedience; it was blind allegiance to authority.

Milgram's study was a stark revelation of our susceptibility to authority's sway. Even when faced with the stark reality of harm inflicted, the pull to obey was overwhelming for many.

This experiment wasn't just a flash in the pan. It ignited a firestorm of debate and introspection in the scientific community. Suddenly, we were forced to confront uncomfortable truths about human behavior and autonomy.

Milgram didn't stop there. He delved deeper, exploring what factors influenced obedience. Peer presence, proximity to authority—both played pivotal roles in shaping our willingness to comply.

The legacy of Milgram's work is undeniable. It's a chilling reminder of the power dynamics at play in society, urging us to question blind allegiance and reclaim our autonomy. Though ethical concerns loom large, the lessons learned from this study continue to reverberate through psychology and beyond, a testament to its enduring impact (Main, 2023).

Solomon Asch's Conformity Experiments

Another landmark study is Solomon Asch's conformity experiments. Asch showed how individuals conform to group opinions, even when they know those opinions are incorrect (Cherry, 2023b).

Imagine stepping into a room for what seems like a simple vision test, surrounded by others. Some of these people are in on the experiment, while you're the unsuspecting subject. Asch's setup involved planting these confederates to see if they could sway your judgment.

In each round, you're shown a line and asked to match it with others of similar length. Seems straightforward, right? But here's where it gets interesting. The catch? Every now and again, the majority of the other participants intentionally give wrong answers. Asch termed these moments the "critical trials" to test if you'd ditch your own perception to blend in with the crowd.

Results were eye-opening. Despite knowing better, a whopping 75% of participants caved in at least once, changing their answer to match the group (Cherry, 2023b). Conformity skyrockets!

Asch discovered a game changer: Introducing just one ally who sticks to the truth drastically reduces conformity. When someone in the group speaks up for what's right, only a small fraction succumbs to the pressure (Cherry, 2023b).

So, why did some buckle? Fear of standing out like a sore thumb, mainly. Many admitted they knew the group was off track but dreaded being the odd one out. Some even started believing the group was onto something.

This experiment highlighted the power of social influence and how manipulators can engineer perceptions to control others.

Stanford Prison Experiment

In 1971, psychologist Philip Zimbardo embarked on a groundbreaking study to dissect the influence of situations versus inherent traits on human behavior. Picture this: 24 young, healthy men, all psychologically stable, were thrown into a mock prison environment, divided randomly into either "prisoners" or "guards" (Mcleod, 2023).

But what ensued was beyond expectation. In just six days, the experiment spiraled out of control, forcing an early termination. The reason? The environment had twisted these men beyond recognition. The pacifist "guards" morphed into sadists, relishing in the humiliation and torment of their fellow participants. Meanwhile, the "prisoners" surrendered their autonomy, blindly following orders and accepting their dehumanization. Even Zimbardo himself, the mastermind behind the study, found himself transformed into an authoritarian figure, embodying the role of the prison superintendent (Mcleod, 2023).

What's the lesson here? Situational forces hold immense power. They can warp the behavior of even the most morally upright individuals. The experiment vividly showcased how good people can be nudged toward darkness when placed in the right (or, rather, wrong) circumstances.

Zimbardo and his team weren't merely satisfying curiosity. They aimed to unravel a pressing question: Were the reported brutalities in

American prisons solely the result of guards' sadistic personalities, or did the environment play a more significant role? In essence, were these guards just inherently aggressive, or did the prison atmosphere trigger their aggression?

The Stanford prison experiment found that the situation and power dynamics affected how people behaved. The guards were mean and bossy, while the prisoners felt sad and obeyed them. The experiment showed how quickly regular people could take on and internalize bad behaviors due to their assigned roles and the environment.

Gaslighting, a key aspect of dark psychology, originated from the 1938 British play *Gas Light* by Patrick Hamilton, which was adapted in 1940 into a British film of the same name. The film was later remade in America in 1944, also titled *Gaslight*, and it's this American version of the film that has since become the main reference for the term. Gaslighting was later explored by psychologists like Theodore Dorpat in the 1980s. Dorpat's research shed light on how manipulators distort reality to undermine their victims' confidence and sanity (Godden, 2008).

Understanding the origins of dark psychology in psychological research helps us recognize the warning signs of manipulation and empowers us to protect ourselves. By being aware of these tactics and their psychological underpinnings, we can develop strategies to safeguard our mental well-being and assert our autonomy in our relationships and interactions with others.

Modern Use of Dark Psychology

In today's world, understanding dark psychology isn't just insightful; it's essential for protecting yourself from manipulation. Dark psychology tactics like gaslighting are not relics of the past or reserved for fictional villains. They're alive and well in contemporary society, lurking in everyday interactions, relationships, and even digital spaces.

Let's dive into how dark psychology manifests in modern life:

- **Social media manipulation:** Ever scrolled through your social media feed and felt inadequate or envious? That's not a coincidence. Dark psychologists exploit social media platforms to manipulate emotions, perceptions, and behaviors. From carefully curated images to targeted ads designed to prey on insecurities, social media is a breeding ground for manipulation.

- **Online scams and cybercrime:** Dark psychology isn't limited to subtle manipulation tactics. It's also at play in the world of cybercrime. Scammers use psychological techniques to deceive and exploit unsuspecting victims online. Whether it's phishing emails preying on fear or fake websites designed to evoke trust, these tactics capitalize on human vulnerabilities.

- **Narcissistic relationships:** Gaslighting, a common tactic in dark psychology, is prevalent in narcissistic relationships. Manipulative individuals use gaslighting to distort reality, making their victims doubt their own perceptions and sanity. In today's dating scene or even within friendships, recognizing and defending ourselves against gaslighting is crucial for maintaining mental well-being.

- **Corporate manipulation:** In the corporate world, dark psychology is often employed to influence consumer behavior or manipulate employees. From deceptive marketing tactics to toxic workplace cultures that erode self-esteem and confidence, the prevalence of dark psychology in business is alarming.

- **Political propaganda and manipulation:** In an era of fake news and echo chambers, political manipulation is rampant. Dark psychology techniques, such as framing, selective exposure, and emotional manipulation, are used to sway public opinion, reinforce biases, and divide communities.

Now, armed with this knowledge of how dark psychology operates in modern society, it's time to take action. Start by sharpening your critical thinking skills and honing your emotional intelligence. Question the information you encounter, both online and offline. Build strong boundaries in your relationships and be wary of individuals who exhibit manipulative behavior. And, most importantly, trust your instincts. If something feels off, don't dismiss it—investigate further.

Implications of Dark Psychology

In the complex world of how people interact, dark psychology is a strong force that includes manipulation, influence, and control. It's not just a vague idea; it's a common reality that affects personal relationships, workplaces, and social groups. However, there is a way to gain strength and protect yourself within this complicated situation.

Consider this: Every interaction carries the potential for manipulation, consciously or subconsciously. Whether it's a subtle guilt trip or a blatant lie, these tactics chip away at our autonomy, leaving us vulnerable and disempowered. But awareness is how we protect ourselves.

Defending yourself against manipulation doesn't mean stooping to the same level. It's about reclaiming your power while maintaining your integrity. It's walking the tightrope of self-preservation without sacrificing your moral compass.

Let's talk about the ethical tightrope. How do you protect yourself without compromising your values? It starts with education and empowerment. Recognizing these tactics for what they are is half the battle won. Armed with knowledge, you can move through these situations with clarity and confidence.

But knowledge alone isn't enough. You need practical tools at your disposal. Think of it as your mental self-defense kit. From setting boundaries to honing your critical thinking skills, each tactic strengthens your shield against manipulation.

Now, let's zoom out for a moment. In our digital age, the battleground has shifted online. Social media, in particular, has become a breeding ground for manipulation and misinformation. Keep in mind that the principles remain the same. Upholding ethical standards in your online interactions is paramount. It's about upholding your integrity among the deceit.

What else is important? Sharing your knowledge and empowering others. By doing this, you create a ripple effect of resilience. Together, we can build a community immune to manipulation, where honesty and respect reign supreme.

You see, dark psychology may be pervasive, but it's not invincible. With awareness, action, and belief in yourself, you can reclaim your autonomy and steer through the complexities of human interaction with confidence and integrity.

Basic Concepts

Several key concepts are fundamental to understanding the principles and applications of dark psychology. Here's an outline of specific concepts, each of which will be covered in depth within their own chapters later in this book:

- **Manipulation:** At its core, manipulation is the art of exerting control over others through subtle, often deceptive means. It's a strategic dance of influence, where individuals seek to shape the thoughts, emotions, and behaviors of others to serve their own agenda. Whether through charm, deception, or coercion, manipulators wield their influence like puppeteers, pulling strings behind the scenes to achieve desired outcomes. Throughout this book, we'll dissect the anatomy of manipulation, exploring its myriad tactics and strategies and empowering you to recognize and resist its insidious allure.

- **Mind control:** This concept delves into the darker recesses of human psychology, where the boundaries between persuasion and coercion blur into obscurity. Mind control encompasses a spectrum of techniques and strategies designed to hijack the very essence of individual autonomy, bending minds to the will of the controller. From subtle forms of persuasion to the depths of hypnotic suggestion, mind control tactics are as varied as they are potent. Through our exploration, you'll gain insight into the mechanics of mind control, learning to fortify your mental defenses against even the most insidious forms of influence.

- **Gaslighting:** A weapon of psychological warfare, gaslighting strikes at the very core of an individual's reality, leaving doubt and confusion in its wake. This subtle form of manipulation seeks to erode a person's sense of self, undermining their perception of reality and sowing seeds of doubt and mistrust. Through a combination of subtle manipulation, denial, and distortion of truth, gaslighters seek to control the narrative, leaving their victims questioning their own sanity. In our exploration, we'll shine a light on the shadowy tactics of gaslighting, equipping you with the tools to recognize and resist its corrosive influence.

- **Psychological warfare:** The battleground of the mind, psychological warfare encompasses a vast array of tactics and strategies aimed at shaping perceptions, influencing behavior, and achieving strategic objectives. From propaganda and misinformation to intimidation and coercion, psychological warfare seeks to exploit vulnerabilities in the human psyche, bending wills and shaping destinies. Through our examination, you'll gain a deeper understanding of the psychological arsenal wielded by manipulators and propagandists, empowering you to navigate the treacherous waters of psychological warfare with clarity and resilience.

Each of these concepts plays a distinct role in the arsenal of dark psychology and will be explored in detail within their respective chapters, providing a comprehensive understanding of their nature, mechanisms, and real-world applications.

Misconceptions

Let's debunk 10 common misconceptions about psychology, manipulation, and related concepts, tying each one back to the insidious tactics of dark psychology:

1. **Misconception: Only the weak-minded fall victim to manipulation.**

   o **Reality:** Manipulation doesn't discriminate based on intelligence or strength. Dark psychology preys on vulnerabilities, exploiting them regardless of mental fortitude.

2. **Misconception: Gaslighting is always obvious.**

   o **Reality:** Gaslighting often begins subtly, with manipulators planting seeds of doubt or subtly twisting the truth. Over time, it can escalate, making it harder to recognize.

3. **Misconception: Manipulators are always outwardly aggressive.**

   o **Reality:** While some manipulators use overt aggression, many operate covertly, employing charm or feigning concern to manipulate emotions and perceptions.

4. **Misconception: Gaslighting only happens in romantic relationships.**

   ○ **Reality:** Gaslighting can occur in any relationship or context, including friendships, family dynamics, and workplace environments. Dark psychology knows no bounds.

5. **Misconception: Victims of manipulation are always aware of it.**

   ○ **Reality:** Manipulators excel at subtlety, often leaving victims unaware of their influence until significant damage has been done. Awareness is a vital step to protection.

6. **Misconception: Manipulation is always intentional.**

   ○ **Reality:** While some manipulators are deliberate in their actions, others may employ manipulative tactics unconsciously, learned from their own experiences or upbringing.

7. **Misconception: Standing up to manipulation always leads to confrontation.**

   ○ **Reality:** Setting boundaries and asserting oneself against manipulation doesn't always result in conflict. In fact, it often fosters healthier relationships built on mutual respect.

8. **Misconception: Once a victim, always a victim.**

   ○ **Reality:** While experiencing manipulation can be traumatic, it doesn't define one's future. With awareness, support, and proactive strategies, individuals can break free from the cycle of manipulation.

9. **Misconception: Manipulation tactics are easy to spot.**

   ○ **Reality:** Dark psychology thrives on subtlety and manipulation tactics that blend seamlessly into everyday interactions. Recognizing these tactics requires keen observation and self-awareness.

10. **Misconception: Victims of manipulation are solely responsible for their predicament.**

    ○ **Reality:** Manipulation places the blame squarely on the shoulders of the manipulator, not the victim. Understanding this empowers individuals to seek help and take proactive steps to protect themselves.

Remember, knowledge is your greatest defense against manipulation. By dispelling these misconceptions and arming yourself with awareness and practical strategies, you can reclaim your autonomy and protect yourself from the insidious tactics of dark psychology.

Interactive Element: The Big Picture

Alright, let's zoom out for a moment and look at the big picture. You've just explored the world of dark psychology. It's like shining a light into the shadows, revealing the strategies that manipulators use to control and exploit others.

This chapter, the "A" in our A.M.E.L.I.O.R.A.T.E. framework, is all about "Accessing dark psychology." It's the crucial first step in our journey toward empowerment and self-protection. By understanding the basic concepts of dark psychology, you're equipping yourself with the tools necessary to understand and deal with human behavior.

Let's tie it all together. As you've learned, dark psychology encompasses a wide array of concepts. These are like arrows in the manipulator's quiver, aimed at destabilizing your sense of reality and control. But, armed with knowledge, you can recognize these tactics for what they are: tools of manipulation.

Now, how does this connect back to our A.M.E.L.I.O.R.A.T.E. framework? Think of it like laying the foundation for a sturdy building. This chapter is the groundwork upon which we'll build our fortress of self-protection. Without a solid understanding of the enemy—dark psychology—you're vulnerable to its insidious influence. But by accessing this knowledge, you're fortifying your defenses and preparing yourself for the battles ahead.

Now that we've wrapped up the first chapter, how are you feeling? Take a deep breath and slow it down for a minute. We've covered a great deal within these pages. The information and pertinent knowledge you are gaining here will contribute to your growth and healing. Take all the time you need to take it all in.

What's up next? We're going to unveil the second step in the A.M.E.L.I.O.R.A.T.E. framework—manipulation. Get ready to gain a better understanding of what it is and how to protect yourself from it.

Chapter 2:

Manipulation—Core Concepts in Psychology

A master manipulator can make you believe that your own thoughts are betraying you. –Friedrich Nietzsche

Welcome to the next phase of our exploration into the intricate workings of dark psychology and the art of manipulation. In this chapter, we're going to look into the second stage of the A.M.E.L.I.O.R.A.T.E framework, focusing on manipulation. Here, we examine the fundamental principles underlying psychological manipulation, equipping you with all you need to know and the strategies necessary to navigate this type of psychological warfare with clarity and confidence.

Dark psychology uses sneaky tactics to influence you without you realizing it. It preys on weaknesses, warps how you see things, and plays with your feelings to get what it wants. Learning about manipulation helps you understand how it works so you can see it coming and not fall for it.

In this chapter, we'll look at how dark psychology and manipulation are connected. We'll explain how these ideas work together by breaking down the basic principles and how manipulation can be dealt with effectively.

Understanding Manipulation as a Psychological Phenomenon

Psychological manipulation is a crafty strategy that some people use to control or influence others. It involves playing mind games to gain power or benefits at the other person's cost. Imagine a situation where one person manipulates another for personal gain, exploiting the other person's vulnerabilities to achieve their own objectives.

One way to identify manipulation is through observing patterns of behavior in relationships. Manipulators often use tactics such as gaslighting or guilt-tripping to control others.

How Manipulation Occurs: The Psychology of Manipulation

Manipulation lurks in the shadows of all relationships, from the intimate bonds of friendship and romance to the familial ties that bind us. Even within the structured confines of the workplace, manipulation can rear its insidious head, often camouflaged by a veneer of normalcy.

Spotting manipulation is not easy. Its subtleties permeate our interactions, leading us to doubt our own perceptions instead of examining the actions of others. Manipulative individuals often employ a repertoire of tactics, each designed to trap their prey. Let's dissect these mechanisms one by one.

Guilt-Tripping

Picture this scenario—a subtle tug at your conscience, a weighty burden placed upon your shoulders. Guilt-tripping, the art of leveraging past favors to extract compliance, is a hallmark maneuver of the manipulative mind. Whether it's a whispered reminder of past sacrifices or a subtle insinuation of indebtedness, the aim remains the same—to bend your will to theirs.

Imagine a situation where a friend continually reminds you of the times they helped you out in the past whenever they need a favor from you—where they subtly imply that you owe them because of their past actions, ultimately trying to influence your decisions through emotional manipulation.

Lying

Lies are what manipulators use. They tell lies to avoid taking responsibility or to control others. Lies lead to manipulation. It can be small lies in daily conversations or big lies that change history. Lies hold manipulation together.

In a romantic relationship, one partner may habitually conceal information or twist the truth to manipulate the other's actions or emotions. For instance, they might lie about their whereabouts or activities to prevent their partner from questioning their loyalty or authority.

In a familial relationship, a manipulative parent might fabricate stories or distort facts to shift blame onto their child for their own shortcomings or mistakes. By deflecting responsibility and casting doubt on their child's integrity, they maintain control and evade accountability.

Flattery

Beware the honeyed words that drip like nectar from the lips of the manipulator. False praise hides hidden motives. Recognize the difference between real compliments and fake flattery used by people trying to get your support.

In a romantic relationship, a manipulative partner may employ excessive flattery to seduce and enthrall their significant other. By lavishing praise on their partner's physical appearance, intelligence, or accomplishments, they aim to cultivate dependency and gain control over their emotions and decisions.

In a professional setting, a manipulative colleague might use flattery as a tool to advance their own agenda. For instance, they might shower their supervisor with exaggerated compliments and admiration to curry favor and secure promotions or favorable treatment, even at the expense of others.

Projection

In the hall of mirrors erected by the manipulative mind, emotions are but mere reflections, distorted and redirected at will. Projection, the act of attributing one's own feelings onto others, serves as both shield and sword for the manipulator. By deflecting accountability and sowing seeds of doubt, they craft a narrative that absolves them of culpability.

In a romantic relationship, a manipulative partner might project their own feelings of insecurity onto their significant other. For example, they may accuse their partner of being untrustworthy or distant when, in reality, it is the manipulator who struggles with trust issues or emotional distance.

In a familial relationship, a manipulative parent may project their own tendencies onto their child. They might accuse their child of being manipulative or deceitful, deflecting attention away from their own controlling behavior and fostering a sense of guilt or self-doubt in the child.

Moving the Goalposts

Think about chasing something that looks real but isn't, like a mirage in the desert. Some people are good at making it impossible for you to meet their standards. They keep changing the rules when you get close to winning. Realize that it's pointless to keep trying and take control of your dreams again.

In a friendship, one person might continuously shift the expectations they have of the other, making it impossible for the friend to meet their demands. For instance, they may initially request occasional help with errands, but as soon as their friend fulfills this request, they raise the bar by demanding more frequent assistance or additional favors. They won't hesitate to remind the friend, "You are never there for me."

In a romantic relationship, one partner might continually change the terms of what they consider to be acceptable behavior, leaving their significant other feeling perpetually inadequate. For example, they may initially express a desire for more quality time together, but once their partner devotes more time to the relationship, they shift the focus to other aspects, such as financial support or physical appearance. The partner may constantly hear, "You are selfish and never consider what I need."

Triangulation

Triangulation is a manipulative technique, often used in interpersonal relationships, where a third party is introduced into a conflict or communication to manipulate or control the dynamic between two individuals. This third party can be anyone from a friend or family member to a colleague or acquaintance. The manipulator typically seeks to create tension, division, or confusion between the original two parties by involving the third party in the interaction.

In a family dynamic, a manipulative parent might engage in triangulation by comparing siblings to each other. For instance, they might praise one sibling for their academic achievements while belittling the other for not measuring up, fostering resentment and competition between the siblings while diverting attention away from their own behavior.

In a romantic relationship, a manipulative partner might triangulate by involving a third party, such as an ex-partner or close friend, in their conflicts with their current partner. By seeking validation or support from this third party, they undermine the trust and intimacy between themselves and their partner, exerting control over the relationship dynamics.

Love Bombing

Beware of excessive displays of affection, because they might hide manipulative intentions. Love bombing, where someone overwhelms you with attention to captivate you, is just the beginning of disappointment. Love bombing is a manipulative tactic used to gain control or influence over another person, typically in a romantic or interpersonal relationship. It involves showering the target with excessive affection, attention, compliments, and gifts to create an intense emotional bond and dependency. The manipulator may use love bombing to quickly establish rapport, gain trust, and elicit feelings of admiration and devotion from the target. However, behind the facade of affection lies a strategic agenda, as the manipulator seeks to exploit the target's vulnerability and manipulate their emotions to serve their own interests. Love bombing can be used as a tool for manipulation, emotional abuse, and control within relationships.

In an established relationship, a manipulative partner might resort to love bombing as a means of reconciliation following a disagreement or conflict. They may flood their partner with apologies, promises of change, and demonstrations of affection, overwhelming them with attention and affection to quell any doubts or resistance. This tactic serves to temporarily alleviate tension and secure their partner's compliance or forgiveness without addressing the underlying issues.

In the face of different forms of manipulation, power comes from knowing and being careful. Equip yourself with the tools to tell who is a friend and who is an enemy, and to tell truth from lies. By staying determined and being committed to protecting yourself, you can make your way through manipulation without harm. Remember, in the fight to keep your mind safe, the biggest win is in being strong and self-aware.

Components of Manipulation

Understanding how people can manipulate you is key. Let's break down manipulation into three components: It involves deceit, lies, and forcing people to do things they might not want to do. It's like a manipulator's toolbox filled with sneaky tricks to control others:

- **Intention:** At the core of manipulation lies intention. It's the driving force behind every deceptive maneuver. When someone pushes an idea or behavior onto another for their own gain, that's manipulation in action. Sadly, this deceptive dance is all too common. Many fall into the trap of exploiting others to satisfy their own desires. Immanuel Kant, the eminent philosopher, dissected this mindset, emphasizing the foundational principle of morality: treating individuals as humans, not mere objects (McCormick, n.d.).

- **Withholding truth:** Manipulation thrives on distortion and concealment of truth. It's about painting a picture that suits the manipulator's agenda, often by exaggerating the benefits of an idea or product. This tactic birthed the Latin warning *caveat emptor*, meaning "buyer beware." In times past, when sellers roamed unchecked, it was a beacon of caution, urging buyers to scrutinize claims before committing. Even today, many have felt the sting of being misled post-purchase. Anything short of transparent honesty is a flagrant act of manipulation (Sayid, 2022).

- **Coercion:** The most blatant component of manipulation is coercion—the brute force of removing free choice, or the "do it or else" ultimatum. Unlike persuasion, which wields influence through free will, coercion shackles individuals to compliance. Any invitation void of the option to decline isn't persuasive but coercive, and is inherently manipulative.

Manipulation, with its trifecta of intention, truth manipulation, and coercion, operates like a silent predator, preying on the unsuspecting. But armed with knowledge, you can repel these insidious tactics, safeguarding your autonomy and well-being.

Additional Types of Emotional Manipulation

Each of these tactics operates insidiously, preying on our vulnerabilities and insecurities. It is in understanding emotional manipulation and recognizing it in action that you can reclaim your power and protect yourself.

Gaslighting

As mentioned, gaslighting, a term born from the 1944 film *Gas Light*, is a quintessential form of emotional manipulation. It stealthily chips away at an individual's grasp on reality, leaving them second-guessing their own perceptions and convictions. Think about it: Have you ever found yourself in a situation where you were made to doubt what you knew to be true?

Meet Erin and Michael, a couple who have been together for several years. Initially, their relationship was filled with love and mutual admiration. However, over time, subtle changes began to emerge.

Michael, once charming and attentive, started displaying behaviors that left Erin feeling confused and unsettled. Whenever she voiced her concerns, Michael would dismiss them, claiming she was "overreacting" or "imagining things."

Initially, Erin brushed off these incidents as misunderstandings or stress. But as they became more frequent, she couldn't shake the feeling that something was wrong. Whenever she tried to talk about her feelings with Michael, he would twist the conversation, making her doubt her own perceptions and memories.

For instance, Erin vividly remembered discussing plans for the weekend with Michael. She suggested spending time together, but Michael vehemently denied ever having such a conversation. He insisted that Erin was "making things up" to stir up trouble. Despite her certainty, Erin found herself questioning her memory and wondering if she had misunderstood the situation.

As gaslighting often does, these incidents slowly eroded Erin's confidence and self-assurance. She began doubting herself in other aspects of their relationship, constantly seeking validation and approval from Michael. Gradually, she became increasingly reliant on him for reassurance, relinquishing control of her reality to him.

What began as subtle manipulation escalated into a toxic cycle of psychological abuse, leaving Erin feeling isolated, confused, and powerless. Gaslighting had effectively undermined her sense of self and reality, trapping her in a relationship characterized by manipulation and control.

This real-life scenario underscores the destructive nature of gaslighting within relationships. It serves as a stark reminder of the importance of recognizing and addressing emotional manipulation early on to protect your mental and emotional well-being.

The Silent Treatment

Imagine that you're in a relationship where everything seemed fine until you did something your partner didn't like. Suddenly, they shut you out completely, refusing to communicate or acknowledge your existence. It's as if you're invisible, left to wonder what you did wrong and desperately seeking their validation.

Mark and Samantha had been dating for a few months and their relationship appeared to be blossoming. They enjoyed spending time together, sharing laughter and creating memories. However, like any couple, they occasionally had a disagreement.

One evening, Mark made plans to hang out with his friends without talking it over with Samantha. When Samantha mentioned she was disappointed, Mark became defensive, insisting that he was entitled to spend time with his friends. Samantha, feeling hurt by Mark's dismissive attitude, tried to explain her feelings, but Mark brushed her off, labeling her as "clingy" and "insecure."

Feeling invalidated and unheard, Samantha withdrew, hoping that Mark would eventually understand her perspective. However, to her dismay,

Mark's behavior only worsened. He stopped responding to her calls and texts, effectively shutting her out of his life.

Days turned into weeks, and Samantha found herself in a state of emotional turmoil. She couldn't understand why Mark was ignoring her or what she had done to warrant such treatment. She replayed their last conversation in her mind, searching for clues or signs of wrongdoing, but everything seemed to blur together.

Feeling invisible and insignificant, Samantha began to question her worth and value in the relationship. She desperately sought Mark's validation, sending dozens of apology texts each day, hoping he would acknowledge her existence and provide reassurance. Yet, no matter how hard she tried, Mark remained distant and unresponsive.

In this scenario, Mark's use of the silent treatment is a classic example of emotional manipulation, specifically designed to control Samantha's behavior and emotions. By withdrawing affection and communication, Mark exerted power over Samantha, leaving her feeling confused, insecure, and desperate for his validation.

This real-life situation highlights the damaging effects of the silent treatment within relationships and underscores the importance of recognizing and addressing emotional manipulation early on. It serves as a poignant reminder that healthy relationships are built on communication, respect, and empathy, not coercion or control.

Emotional Security

In a workplace setting, your supervisor consistently undermines your efforts, belittling your accomplishments and making you feel incompetent. Despite your best efforts, you find yourself constantly questioning your capabilities, perpetually seeking approval and validation from others.

Meet Jessie, a diligent and hardworking employee who prides herself on her professional capabilities. She has been working in a marketing firm for several years, where she consistently exceeds expectations and delivers exceptional results. However, despite her efforts, Jessie finds herself caught in a web of emotional manipulation orchestrated by her supervisor, John.

John has a habit of undermining Jessie's efforts and belittling her accomplishments. During team meetings, John often dismisses Jessie's ideas, labeling them as impractical or irrelevant. He takes credit for her successes, claiming them as his own, while publicly criticizing her mistakes and shortcomings.

Despite Jessie's best efforts to maintain her confidence and composure, John's relentless criticism takes a toll on her self-esteem. She begins to doubt her capabilities and second-guess her decisions, constantly seeking approval and validation from her colleagues and superiors.

In one instance, Jessie spends weeks meticulously planning a marketing campaign, pouring her heart and soul into every detail. However, when she presents her ideas to John, he immediately shoots them down, citing vague reasons and offering no constructive feedback. Jessie feels deflated and demoralized, wondering if she's truly as competent as she once believed.

As time goes on, Jessie finds herself in a perpetual cycle of seeking validation and approval from others, fearing that she will never be good enough in John's eyes. Despite receiving praise and recognition from other colleagues, Jessie remains fixated on gaining John's approval, believing that her worth as an employee hinges on his validation.

This example shows us how emotional manipulation tactics can be used to exert control and undermine confidence in the workplace. By belittling accomplishments and fostering self-doubt, a toxic work environment is created where the employee feels powerless and inadequate.

Aggressive Sense of Humor

Imagine being in a group where one person habitually uses humor as a weapon, ridiculing others under the guise of jest. They target your insecurities and vulnerabilities, all while laughing it off as harmless banter. But deep down, you're left feeling humiliated and self-conscious, unsure whether to laugh along or confront their hurtful behavior.

Shaming

Whether it's body shaming, career shaming, or any other form, shaming tactics cut deep, leaving scars that may never fully heal. Consider a scenario where a family member constantly criticizes your life choices, making you feel inadequate and unworthy of love and acceptance.

Implicit Threats

Picture a manipulative boss who subtly hints at the dire consequences of not complying with their demands. They may not spell it out explicitly, but the underlying message is clear—obey or face the repercussions.

Criticism

Constructive criticism can be valuable for personal and professional growth, but relentless criticism aimed at breaking down your self-esteem is a different story. Imagine a partner who habitually nitpicks everything you do, leaving you feeling worthless and unlovable.

Susan and her teenage daughter Christine shared a close bond, but as Christine entered her adolescent years, their relationship began to show signs of strain. Susan, a perfectionist by nature, had high expectations for Christine's academic performance and behavior.

Every day after school, Susan would meticulously inspect Christine's homework assignments, pointing out every minor mistake and oversight. No matter how hard Christine tried, it seemed like she could never meet her mother's standards.

If Christine forgot to dot an "i" or cross a "t," Susan would launch into a tirade of criticism, chastising her for her carelessness and lack of attention to detail. Over time, Christine's self-esteem began to plummet, and she started doubting her abilities and worth as a person. It took a toll on her mental health, leaving her feeling worthless and unlovable. Christine dreaded coming home from school, knowing that she would inevitably face her mother's relentless criticism.

Susan's habit of criticizing everything Christine did had a detrimental effect on her daughter's self-esteem and well-being. Relentless criticism aimed at breaking down self-esteem only serves to damage relationships and undermine confidence.

Blackmail

It's the ultimate power play—using sensitive information or secrets to coerce compliance. Whether it's threatening to expose a hidden truth or using past mistakes as leverage, blackmail instills fear and obedience in its victims.

Emily and Lisa had been best friends since childhood, sharing everything from secrets to dreams. However, their friendship took a dark turn when Emily discovered that Lisa had been spreading rumors about her behind her back.

Feeling betrayed and hurt, Emily confronted Lisa, demanding an explanation for her actions. Instead of apologizing, Lisa turned the tables on Emily, threatening to reveal a secret from Emily's past that she had confided in her years ago.

Terrified of the potential consequences, Emily begged Lisa to keep her secret, pleading with her not to expose her vulnerabilities to the world. Lisa, relishing her newfound power over Emily, used the threat of blackmail to coerce Emily into compliance, forcing her to remain silent about Lisa's betrayal.

Fearing the fallout of her secret being exposed, Emily reluctantly agreed to Lisa's demands, sacrificing her own dignity and self-respect to protect herself from humiliation and shame.

Lisa's use of blackmail as a power play illustrates the destructive nature of manipulation and coercion. By exploiting sensitive information and secrets, Lisa instilled fear and obedience in Emily, effectively controlling her actions and emotions for her own gain.

Isolation

Emotional manipulators often seek to control their victims by cutting them off from external support systems. Picture a partner who systematically alienates you from other social circles, leaving you dependent on their approval and validation for a sense of belonging.

Jack and Rachel had been in a relationship for a few years, and things had started off wonderfully. They enjoyed spending time together, sharing inside jokes , and creating a life together. However, as their relationship progressed, Jack's behavior took a strange turn.

At first, it was subtle. Jack would express disapproval whenever Rachel wanted to spend time with her friends or family. He would make snide remarks about her social circle, insinuating that they were a bad influence on her or that they didn't truly care about her.

Slowly but surely, Jack started to distance Rachel from her support systems. He would guilt-trip her whenever she wanted to go out with friends, accusing her of neglecting their relationship or prioritizing others over him. Over time, Rachel found herself making excuses to her friends and family, opting to stay home with Jack instead of maintaining her social connections.

As Jack's grip tightened, Rachel's world grew smaller. She became increasingly isolated, dependent on Jack's approval and validation for a sense of belonging. Without the support of her friends and family, Rachel felt trapped in a relationship where her worth was contingent on Jack's approval.

Jack's systematic alienation of Rachel from her social circles illustrates the insidious nature of emotional manipulation. By cutting her off from her external support systems, Jack effectively controlled Rachel's behavior and emotions, leaving her isolated and dependent on him for validation and belonging.

Blaming

In manipulative relationships, accountability becomes a one-way street. Imagine a partner who habitually shifts blame onto you for their own mistakes and shortcomings, leaving you feeling guilty and responsible for their actions.

Mia and Alex had been together for a few years, and while their relationship had its ups and downs, Mia always tried to make things work. However, there was a troubling pattern that emerged whenever conflicts arose.

Whenever something went wrong, whether it was a forgotten anniversary or a financial setback, Alex would immediately shift the blame onto Mia. He would accuse her of being careless or irresponsible, insisting that she was the cause of their problems.

Even when Mia tried to reason with Alex or point out his own role in the situation, he would dismiss her concerns, refusing to take any responsibility for his actions. Instead, he would continue to blame Mia, making her feel guilty and responsible for their relationship's shortcomings.

Over time, Mia began to internalize Alex's accusations, believing that she was indeed the cause of their problems. She would constantly second-guess herself, wondering if she was truly to blame for everything that went wrong in their relationship.

As the cycle of blame continued, Mia found herself trapped in a toxic dynamic where accountability ran in only one direction. No matter how hard she tried to communicate or resolve their issues, Alex's refusal to acknowledge his own mistakes left Mia feeling helpless and alone.

Alex's habit of shifting blame onto Mia illustrates the damaging effects of manipulation in a relationship. By refusing to take accountability for his actions, Alex undermined Mia's self-esteem and perpetuated a cycle of guilt and self-doubt, leaving her feeling responsible for his shortcomings.

Data Manipulation

With the rise of technology, data manipulation has become an increasingly prevalent form of emotional manipulation. Imagine a scenario where someone distorts information or selectively presents facts to sway your opinions or manipulate your emotions.

Meet Mark, a college student who's passionate about environmental conservation. He's actively involved in advocating for sustainable practices in his community and frequently shares articles and information about climate change on social media.

One day, Mark comes across a compelling article claiming that renewable energy sources are ineffective and costly. The article is filled with statistics and graphs seemingly proving its point. Intrigued, Mark shares the article with his friends, hoping to spark a discussion about alternative energy solutions.

However, unbeknownst to Mark, the article was carefully crafted to manipulate readers' emotions and sway their opinions. Upon closer examination, Mark discovers that the data presented in the article has been cherry-picked to support a biased narrative.

Feeling betrayed and misled, Mark realizes that he has inadvertently contributed to the spread of misinformation. He's frustrated by the realization that his genuine efforts to raise awareness about environmental issues were hijacked by those seeking to manipulate public opinion for their own agenda.

Determined to combat data manipulation and misinformation, Mark redoubles his efforts to verify sources and critically evaluate information before sharing it online. He becomes an advocate for media literacy and encourages others to question the validity of the information presented to them, recognizing the power of data manipulation in shaping public discourse.

Differentiating Manipulation

Influence vs. Manipulation

Let's look a little deeper into the world of psychological manipulation and distinguish between influence and manipulation. It's essential to grasp the nuances between the two, as they operate on different ethical and psychological grounds.

- **Influence**

    o   Influence stems from the genuine desire to persuade or guide someone toward a certain decision or behavior.

    o   It often involves transparency, honesty, and ethical persuasion tactics.

    o   Influencers aim to inspire positive change or encourage individuals to adopt certain beliefs or behaviors that align with their own.

- **Manipulation**

    o   Manipulation, on the other hand, is rooted in deceit, coercion, and exploitation.

    o   It involves cunning strategies aimed at controlling or exploiting others for personal gain.

    o   Manipulators often employ deceptive tactics, emotional manipulation, or psychological coercion to achieve their objectives.

- **The fine line**

    - Influence operates within ethical boundaries, respecting the autonomy and free will of individuals.

    - Manipulation, however, disregards ethical considerations, seeking to subvert or override the autonomy of others for selfish motives.

Distinguishing Characteristics

Influence typically arises from a genuine desire to guide or persuade, driven by noble intentions. Manipulation is driven by self-serving motives, with the intent to exploit or control others for personal gain.

Influence is often transparent, with influencers openly expressing their intentions and providing relevant information. Manipulation thrives in secrecy, often concealing ulterior motives or employing deceptive tactics to mislead the target.

Empowerment vs. Exploitation

Influence empowers individuals by providing them with information, guidance, and support to make informed decisions. On the other hand, manipulation exploits vulnerabilities, undermines confidence, and fosters dependency to exert control over the target.

Protecting Yourself

Educate yourself about the tactics and red flags associated with manipulation. Be vigilant for subtle coercive techniques aimed at undermining your autonomy or emotional well-being. Trust your intuition and gut feelings when something feels off or manipulative; don't dismiss your concerns or doubts, even if they seem irrational at first glance. Establish clear boundaries and assertively communicate them to others. Refuse to engage with individuals who disregard your boundaries or employ manipulative tactics. Nurture your sense of self-worth and autonomy and cultivate critical thinking skills and independent decision-making to resist manipulation attempts.

While influence and manipulation may share superficial similarities, their underlying motives and methods diverge significantly. By understanding the distinctions between the two, you empower yourself to navigate interpersonal dynamics with clarity and resilience, safeguarding your psychological well-being against manipulation's insidious grasp.

Features of Overt Manipulation

In its simplest form, "overt" signifies what is apparent or visible to the naked eye. Overt manipulation involves behaviors that are clearly observable, reflecting the inner thoughts or intentions of the manipulator and evident to those around them. In other words, the abuser isn't trying to hide their behavior.

Overt behaviors can harm relationships by breaking trust and intimacy. Abusive behaviors, on the other hand, involve consistently downplaying others' feelings and experiences to control them. For example, an abusive parent may purposely make their child feel unworthy to keep them dependent and obedient.

Overt abuse is when someone clearly shows aggressive behavior that is easy to understand. This can include things like slamming doors, yelling, angry looks, name-calling, stomping feet, or making disrespectful gestures. The purpose of this behavior is to show power and make the other person afraid.

Characteristics of Covert Manipulation

Covert manipulation happens secretly in the shadows, using psychological tricks that are sneaky and harmful. It involves deceiving others with a charming facade to hide one's true motives. How is covert manipulation different from overt manipulation, and how can we spot these secretive tactics?

At its core, covert manipulation is all about being sneaky, hiding one's true intentions behind unclear messages and the ability to deny involvement. Unlike obvious manipulation, which is easy to spot and leaves little room for doubt, covert manipulation works beneath the surface, subtly influencing our thoughts, feelings, and actions without us even realizing it.

Imagine a scenario where a romantic partner showers you with affection and attention, only to gradually undermine your self-confidence and independence over time. Their manipulative tactics are so covertly executed that you find yourself questioning your own perceptions and reality, trapped in a web of gaslighting and emotional manipulation.

Manipulation can take different forms, all meant to exploit our weaknesses and undermine our confidence. It might show up as subtle guilt trips, where the manipulator makes you doubt yourself or feel like you owe them something. Alternatively, it could be passive-aggressive behavior, where the manipulator indirectly shows hostility or anger, making you feel unsure and unimportant.

What sets covert manipulation apart is its ability to masquerade as genuine concern or care, making it all the more difficult to detect and resist. Unlike overt manipulation, which relies on open displays of power and control, covert manipulation operates through deception and manipulation, undermining our autonomy and agency in subtle yet profound ways. These master manipulators will always appear to others as "great" or "wonderful," willing to do anything for anyone. They hide their true selves from those not under their control.

Awareness is our greatest ally, empowering us to recognize the subtle signs of manipulation and trust our instincts. By understanding how to set and maintain healthy boundaries, we can safeguard our emotional well-being.

Interactive Element: The Big Picture

Alright, let's zoom back out and look at the big picture. How often do we find ourselves unwittingly caught in the web of manipulation, unsure of how we got there or how to escape?

Returning to the A.M.E.L.I.O.R.A.T.E. framework, we revisit the second stage: Manipulation. Here, we confront the harsh reality that manipulation is not merely a theoretical concept but a pervasive force in our daily lives. It infiltrates our relationships, workplaces, and even our own minds, shaping our actions and beliefs without us even realizing it.

But, armed with knowledge, we can turn the tide. The strategies laid out in this chapter offer a map to move through the treacherous terrain of manipulation. By understanding the tactics employed by manipulators, we reclaim our agency and empower ourselves to resist their influence.

Let's connect the dots: Each insight into dark psychology serves as a building block within the A.M.E.L.I.O.R.A.T.E. framework. By recognizing manipulation for what it is, we take a vital step toward self-protection and personal growth.

Reiterate to yourself: The goal here is not merely to dwell on the darkness but to emerge stronger, wiser, and more resilient. By applying the insights gleaned from this chapter, we take a proactive stance in safeguarding our mental well-being and preserving our autonomy.

In closing, remember that what we learn here is how we will protect ourselves and grow. As we continue our journey through the A.M.E.L.I.O.R.A.T.E. framework, let us do so with conviction, knowing that each stride brings us closer to a life unburdened by the shadows of manipulation.

It's time to turn the page and dive into the next stage of the framework, "Exploring the techniques road map."

Chapter 3:

Exploring the Techniques Road Map

Manipulation is the shadow that lurks behind every human interaction. –Sigmund Freud

We are now entering the third phase of the A.M.E.L.I.O.R.A.T.E. framework: "Exploring the techniques road map." Here, we will be unearthing the nefarious techniques employed by manipulators to control, deceive, and exploit unsuspecting minds.

Have you ever found yourself second-guessing your own thoughts, feelings, or memories? Have you experienced the unsettling sensation of being manipulated without even realizing it?

These are the subtle signs of psychological manipulation, a crafty game played by those who seek power and domination over others.

By the end of this chapter, you will emerge with a deeper understanding of the basic psychological manipulation tactics at play, equipping you with the tools needed to move through this terrain with clarity and confidence.

Overview of Common Manipulation Tactics

Manipulation in Communication

When we look more closely at manipulative communication, the landscape of our relationships—both personal and professional—can quickly become treacherous waters. It's not the outcome anyone desires, yet it's a reality many face. Manipulative communication, driven by self-serving motives, corrodes the foundation of trust, leaving behind a wake of discord and disillusionment. Armed with awareness and strategic action, you can maneuver through these depths unscathed, preserving trust and integrity.

Consider how it feels when someone hijacks a conversation with manipulative tactics. The frustration, the sense of being trapped, the indignation—it's like being treated as a mere pawn in someone else's game. But here's the crux: You have the power to break free from this cycle. Recognize the signs of manipulative communication, both in others and within yourself, and seize control of the narrative.

Let's dissect some common manipulative tactics in communication and craft strategies to counteract them:

- **Statements disguised as questions:** Ever encountered the seemingly innocent inquiry, "I'm sure you agree?" Don't be deceived. It's a veiled attempt at assertion, not a genuine inquiry. This person is hiding their statement in a manipulative manner inside this question and has zero interest in what you honestly think. How can I be sure? They would have asked the question, "So, what do you think?" To sidestep it, pivot toward authentic dialogue. Ask real questions in return and invite genuine participation and exchange of ideas. For example, if someone says, "I'm sure you agree," you can follow with, "Oh, are you asking my opinion on this?"

- **Absolutes:** When someone directs negative absolute phrases toward you—phrases like "You never" or "You always"—it's a manipulated ploy to elicit a defensive response. These statements are designed to corner you, making you feel compelled to defend your character. It's a subtle form of control, chipping away at your trust in yourself. But here's the antidote: Refuse to accept these absolutes as gospel truth. Recognize them for what they are—manipulative tactics aimed at undermining your confidence. Instead of falling into the trap of defense, challenge the absolutist assertions. Assert that absolutes rarely hold true in complex human interactions. Then, pivot the conversation to specifics. Encourage the manipulator to provide concrete examples that can be examined and discussed objectively. For example, if this person says, "You are never there for me," you respond with, "I'm sorry you feel that way—can you please tell me a time this happened?" By refusing to engage in the defensive dance orchestrated by manipulative communication, you reclaim your power and uphold the integrity of your interactions.

- **Appeal to authority:** The tactic of leveraging data, facts, or supposed consensus to bolster one's argument is a classic maneuver in the manipulator's playbook. Resist the temptation to wield vague claims as weapons. Embrace transparency and substantiate your assertions with concrete evidence.

- **Gossip and lying:** Engaging in gossip, whether grounded in truth or in fabrication, is a form of manipulation that corrodes trust. Reject the notion that it's an inherent aspect of human nature. Refuse to participate in spreading rumors, and challenge others who attempt to draw you into their web of deceit. As for lying, it's the ultimate betrayal of trust. Commit to honesty, even when the truth is uncomfortable.

In the face of manipulation, employ a strategic approach: Deconstruct the web of falsehoods and half-truths, unraveling each strand to dismantle its power. This technique of dissecting manipulation into its constituent parts is a potent tool in your toolkit.

Remember, manipulation thrives in the shadows of ignorance and complacency. Arm yourself with knowledge, cultivate discernment, and reclaim agency over your interactions. By doing so, you fortify your defenses against psychological warfare, preserving the sanctity of trust and authenticity in your relationships.

Psychological Exploitation

Psychological exploitation is the art of manipulating someone's thoughts, emotions, and behaviors for personal gain or control. It's a dark realm where perpetrators prey on vulnerabilities, twisting perceptions and distorting reality to serve their own agendas. But understanding the commonly employed tactics and recognizing them is your first line of defense.

Deceptive Communication Strategies

Verbal Manipulation Techniques

Language holds immense power, doesn't it? With mere words, we can bridge gaps, seek understanding, offer comfort. Yet, within those very words also lies the potential for distance, misunderstanding, and pain. It's a double-edged sword, isn't it? Verbal manipulation, subtle and insidious, can permeate our relationships, leaving us grappling with dissatisfaction and frustration. But spotting it isn't always a walk in the park. How do we distinguish between a heated debate and manipulation, especially when it involves someone close to us?

Let's delve into five common forms of verbal manipulation:

- **Retention and silence as tools of control:** Ever experienced the silent treatment? It's not just a petty annoyance; it's a tactic wielded to induce guilt and compliance. When one party withholds information or resorts to monosyllables, they're erecting barriers in communication, pushing the other into a psychological no-man's-land. For example, a friend asks your opinion on her new relationship. You are honest and confide in her that you feel he may be a bit too controlling for her. You mention that you are genuinely concerned. Your friend is immediately upset with you, and you can feel the tension. Despite trying to reach out for days, you hear nothing back.

- **Dialogue blockade to sustain conflict:** Imagine a looming conflict, but certain topics are off-limits. By cherry-picking conversation topics, one party keeps the tension simmering, like an unspoken elephant in the room. The victim, wary of repercussions, tiptoes around the issue, perpetuating the imbalance of power. Let's say you've been together with your partner for years, but lately, tensions have been mounting. There's an issue—your partner's frequent nights out with friends. You've tried bringing it up, but every time you do so, your partner changes the subject. You end up talking about work, hobbies, anything but the real issue at hand. You, sensing the tension, tiptoe around the topic, fearing another argument. Meanwhile, your partner controls the conversation, steering it away from uncomfortable territory, leaving you feeling unheard and powerless. The unresolved issue lingers beneath the surface, casting a shadow over your relationship. Your partner's selective conversation topics create a barrier to addressing the underlying conflict, perpetuating a power imbalance where your concerns are sidelined.

- **Blame and criticism as weapons:** Nothing like a good blame game to keep you on your toes, right? Manipulators excel at pointing fingers, even for their own shortcomings. Through relentless criticism, they chip away at your self-esteem, leaving you vulnerable and pliable to their whims. Ever had one of those small arguments with your partner that blows up into something much bigger? Did it leave you confused? Did you mention that you asked them to take out the garbage and now you're sitting there scratching your head because they're insisting you never asked? Are they now blaming you not only for the garbage but also for being controlling and demanding? Welcome to the blame game.

- **Denial of responsibility:** Owning up to mistakes? Not in the manipulator's playbook. Denial shifts the blame elsewhere, refusing to acknowledge the consequences of their actions. By shirking responsibility, they leave the victim carrying the weight of the relationship's issues alone. A classic example of this one? When a partner cheats yet shifts blame by saying, "Well if you met my needs, if you were nicer, if you cooked more, I wouldn't have cheated."

- **Trivialization of feelings:** Ever had your emotions belittled or dismissed? It's a classic manipulation tactic. By downplaying the significance of your feelings or ideas, the other party undermines your emotional reality. You're left questioning the validity of your own experiences, inching closer to self-doubt. For example, you come home after a really bad day at work and your partner finds you crying. Instead of them asking what's wrong or how they can help, you're faced with, "Are you crying again? You should grow up."

Detecting verbal manipulation is key, but it's no easy feat. Watch out for red flags— escalating conflicts, recurring dissatisfaction. If communication strays from assertiveness, it's time to hit pause. Someone might be leveraging conflict for personal gain. Awareness is your armor, empowering you to navigate the murky waters of manipulation. So, stay vigilant, and remember—your voice matters.

Nonverbal Manipulation Strategies

Let's explore the covert world of nonverbal manipulation strategies, where actions speak louder than words. These techniques are subtle yet potent tools wielded to influence behavior, opinions, and decisions. Whether you're on the receiving end or contemplating their use, understanding these tactics is key to understanding human interaction:

- **Body language mirroring:** Have you ever noticed someone unconsciously mimicking your gestures, posture, or facial expressions? This mirroring technique builds rapport and fosters a sense of connection by signaling similarity and empathy. It's a powerful way to establish trust and subtly guide others toward alignment with your perspective. Pay attention to whether someone mirrors your movements—it could reveal their attempt to influence you, or their receptiveness to your influence.

- **Eye contact manipulation:** The eyes are windows to the soul—and to subtle manipulation. Maintaining prolonged eye contact can convey confidence, sincerity, and dominance. Conversely, breaking eye contact at strategic moments can instill doubt, discomfort, or submission. Be mindful of the intentions behind someone's gaze—is it a genuine attempt to connect or a calculated ploy to assert control?

- **Proxemics:** The use of space can speak volumes about power dynamics and intentions. Invading someone's personal space can evoke feelings of discomfort or intimidation, while maintaining a comfortable distance fosters a sense of respect and autonomy. Pay attention to how individuals navigate physical proximity in different contexts—it can reveal underlying agendas and power struggles.

- **Gestures and posture:** Our body language communicates volumes, often without us even realizing it. Open, expansive gestures convey confidence and assertiveness, while closed, constricted postures signal defensiveness or submission. Pay attention to the subtle cues in how others carry themselves— are they projecting strength or masking vulnerability?

- **Microexpressions:** The fleeting expressions that flit across our faces can betray our true feelings, even when we try to conceal them. Learning to recognize microexpressions—such as a subtle flash of contempt or a fleeting smirk—can provide valuable insights into someone's true intentions and emotions. Pay attention to these subtle cues—they may reveal more than words ever could.

Armed with an understanding of these nonverbal manipulation strategies, you're better equipped to navigate the intricate dance of human interaction. Whether you're seeking to influence others or shield yourself from manipulation, awareness is your most potent weapon. Stay vigilant, trust your instincts, and remember: Actions speak louder than words.

Emotional Manipulation Techniques

Understanding Emotional Triggers

Emotional manipulation is a subtle yet insidious form of psychological warfare, and at its core lies the concept of emotional triggers. But what exactly is an emotional trigger and why do they hold such power over us?

An emotional trigger is essentially a psychological button that, when pressed, evokes a strong emotional response within us. These triggers can stem from past experiences, traumas, fears, or deeply ingrained beliefs. They act as access points for manipulators to exploit and control our emotions.

Imagine that you're in a heated argument with someone and they say something that instantly makes your blood boil. Maybe they say you're a bad mother or bring up a private incident from your childhood. That's your emotional trigger being activated. It could be a word, a tone of voice, or a certain behavior that instantly transports you back to a time when you felt hurt, angry, or vulnerable.

Understanding your emotional triggers is crucial because it allows you to regain control over your emotional responses. It's like shining a light into the dark corners of your mind and uncovering the root causes of your reactions.

So, how do you identify your emotional triggers? Start by paying attention to your emotional responses in different situations. Notice patterns in your reactions. What situations or words tend to set you off? Once you've identified your triggers, take the time to explore why they affect you so deeply. What past experiences or beliefs are connected to them?

Once you've gained clarity on your emotional triggers, you can begin to disarm them. This doesn't mean ignoring or suppressing your emotions; it means understanding them and consciously choosing how to respond. Practice self-awareness and self-regulation techniques such as mindfulness, deep breathing, or cognitive reframing to help you stay calm and centered when faced with triggering situations.

Moreover, be vigilant of how others may attempt to exploit your emotional triggers. Manipulators are skilled at identifying and using these vulnerabilities to their advantage. By understanding your triggers, you can better protect yourself from emotional manipulation and maintain your autonomy.

In essence, understanding emotional triggers is the first step in reclaiming your emotional sovereignty. It empowers you to navigate the murky waters of psychological manipulation with clarity and resilience. So, take the time to delve into your psyche, unearth your triggers, and arm yourself with knowledge to safeguard your emotional well-being.

How You Can Use a Trigger to Your Advantage

How can we harness the power of emotional triggers to safeguard ourselves against manipulation and even turn the tables?

Let's talk strategy. Imagine you're in a situation where someone is attempting to manipulate you. They're trying to exploit your vulnerabilities, your fears, your insecurities. But here's where it gets interesting: What if you anticipated their moves? What if you knew exactly which buttons they were trying to push?

That's where self-awareness comes into play. Take a deep dive into your own psyche. What makes you tick? What sets you off? By identifying your emotional triggers, you're essentially disarming your opponent before they even make a move.

Once you've mastered the art of self-awareness, it's time to play offense. Use your knowledge of emotional triggers to your advantage. When you sense someone trying to manipulate you, flip the script. Take control of the situation. Instead of reacting emotionally, respond strategically.

For example, if someone tries to use guilt to manipulate you, recognize it for what it is—a tactic. Then, calmly assert your boundaries. Don't let them push you around. By staying grounded and composed, you're robbing them of their power.

Emotional triggers aren't just a defensive tool. They're also a source of strength. Think about it: What if you could harness the power of positive emotions to inspire and motivate yourself? What if you could turn your passions and desires into driving forces for success?

That's the beauty of emotional intelligence. It's not just about avoiding manipulation; it's about harnessing the full spectrum of human emotion to achieve your goals and fulfill your potential.

Exploiting Emotional Vulnerabilities

Your emotions, raw and unguarded, are like open wounds waiting to be exploited. But how does this exploitation unfold and what makes it so insidious?

First, understand this: Emotional vulnerabilities are the chinks in your psychological armor, the soft spots where manipulation finds its entry point. They can stem from past traumas, insecurities, fears, or unmet needs. Perpetrators of dark psychology wield these vulnerabilities like weapons, probing for weaknesses to exploit and manipulate you.

Imagine someone who knows your deepest insecurities, your fears, your desires. They use this knowledge to craft their narrative, to twist reality in their favor. It's not just about pushing your buttons; it's about reprogramming your perceptions, distorting your reality until you're dancing to their tune without even realizing it.

Now, let's break it down further. Gaslighting, a favorite tactic of emotional manipulators, thrives on exploiting your emotional vulnerabilities. As they gradually erode your sanity, a subtle manipulation leaves you questioning your own reality. They might undermine your confidence, cause doubt, or even outright deny events that you know to be true. And each time you lose your sense of self, your emotional vulnerabilities become their playground.

When you understand how emotional vulnerabilities are exploited, you can reclaim that power for yourself. Start by identifying your own vulnerabilities. What are the wounds from your past that still ache? What are the insecurities that gnaw at your confidence? By shining a light on these vulnerabilities, you rob them of their power to control you.

Let me tell you the quick story of Mikayla. She dated a man for eight years before marrying him. They stayed married for 18 years and had three children together. Mikayla noticed the manipulative behavior in the third year of marriage, and it continued to get worse as the years went on. Her husband would eventually tell her what to wear (by convincing her he wanted her to look amazing), what friends to have (by convincing her he had her best interests in mind), and that he didn't want her working (by convincing her that staying home with their children was best). Mikayla soon realized, as her children grew, that she needed to be a better example for them. She got into therapy and had help uncovering her vulnerabilities. This brought her power. Once she knew her own weaknesses, it took her husband's power away. No longer could he push her buttons. Divorce would follow, and Mikayla's healing did as well.

Next, fortify your defenses. Surround yourself with a support network of trusted friends and family who can provide a reality check when you need it most. Practice self-care and self-compassion, nurturing your emotional resilience so that manipulation finds no fertile ground to take root.

And finally, trust your instincts. If something feels off, if your gut is screaming at you that you're being manipulated, listen to that voice. Don't dismiss it or rationalize it away. Your intuition is your most powerful weapon against emotional manipulation.

So, in the battlefield of dark psychology, remember this: Your emotions may be vulnerabilities, but they are also your greatest strength. By understanding them, protecting them, and trusting them, you can navigate the minefield of manipulation with clarity and resilience.

Interactive Element: The Big Picture

Imagine a world where your mind is a battleground, where unseen forces seek to manipulate your thoughts, emotions, and behaviors without your awareness. This is where the art of manipulation reaches its darkest depths. By understanding these tactics, you gain the power to defend yourself against their insidious influence.

Let's zoom out and grasp the big picture. Dark psychology is not just a collection of sinister techniques; it's a comprehensive system of manipulation designed to exploit vulnerabilities in human psychology.

But in the shadows, there is light. Enter the A.M.E.L.I.O.R.A.T.E. framework—hope in the darkness. Remember, you are the master of your own destiny, so arm yourself with knowledge, fortify your defenses, and claim the victory that is rightfully yours.

Throughout this chapter, we've looked deep into the dark recesses of psychology, exploring the insidious tactics of manipulation.

But knowledge alone is not enough. It's what you do with this knowledge that truly empowers you. Armed with the insights gained here, you possess the ability to recognize manipulation tactics as they unfold and to safeguard your mental and emotional well-being.

In the next chapter, we look into the covert techniques employed by master manipulators, equipping you with the tools to not only defend against their tactics but also gain insight into the inner workings of the human psyche. Get ready to uncover the secrets of leading covert techniques in dark psychology as we continue our journey toward enlightenment and empowerment.

Chapter 4:

Leading Covert Techniques in

Dark Psychology

To truly understand dark psychology, one must be willing to explore the darkest corners of the human mind. –Philip Zimbardo

The fourth phase of the A.M.E.L.I.O.R.A.T.E. framework, "Leading covert techniques in dark psychology," is a vital component of this journey. Understanding these techniques isn't just about recognizing them; it's about arming yourself with the knowledge to resist and counteract them. By the end of this chapter, you'll not only be able to spot the signs of manipulation but also have the tools to protect yourself and reclaim your agency.

Exploration of Covert Manipulation

Covert manipulation lurks in the shadows, a dark art employed by those craving power and control over others. It's the subtle poison that seeps into your consciousness, altering your thoughts, actions, and perceptions without you even realizing it. Imagine being held captive not by physical restraints but by the intricate web of deceit woven by a skilled manipulator.

But how do you recognize the signs? How do you know if you're falling prey to these covert tactics? The truth is, it's not always easy. You might sense something's off—a nagging feeling, a gut instinct—but you can't quite put your finger on it. That's because manipulators are masters at reading you, exploiting you, and using your fears and desires with surgical precision.

Meet Mark, who was swept off his feet by someone who seemed like the embodiment of his dreams. In a very short amount of time, they showered him with affection, compliments, and promises of a future together. Mark was wrapped up in the intoxicating, exhilarating fever of it all. He had no idea that behind this facade of love was a darker agenda.

Despite the odd red flag and comments from close friends, Mark convinced himself that this relentless barrage of positivity and love was genuine. He was not aware of the strategic move that was being meticulously crafted to hook him in, to make him vulnerable to the manipulation that would inevitably follow.

Mark watched the honeymoon phase fade and the dynamics of the relationship shift. Suddenly, he found himself tiptoeing around his partner, constantly questioning his worth and sanity. Those closest to Mark watched as his partner alternated between the charming person he first met and the cruel tormentor who was chipping away at his self-esteem. Mark would lie awake at night wondering how the fairy tale had turned into a nightmare.

The answer lies in the insidious nature of covert manipulation. It's the puppet strings pulled from the shadows, leaving you bewildered and broken.

The Intricacies of Covert Strategies

Let's delve into the intricate world of covert manipulation, where psychological warfare operates beneath the surface, targeting our vulnerabilities and twisting our perceptions. In this realm, understanding the dark arts of manipulation isn't just insightful; it's crucial for safeguarding our mental well-being and autonomy:

- **Social manipulation (social scalping):** Imagine a scenario where someone inflates their own worth while subtly diminishing yours—a classic case of social scalping. This insidious tactic exploits the basic principle of reciprocity, where indebtedness fosters a sense of obligation. The social scalper, adept at their craft, employs various techniques: presenting favors as exclusive, exaggerating their costliness, or reminding you of past deeds. Through these maneuvers, they aim to extract more than they give, leaving you unwittingly indebted.

- **Pity plays:** Picture someone painting themselves as a helpless victim, tugging at your heartstrings to elicit pity. This is the pity play—a manipulation tactic intertwined with guilt-tripping. By positioning themselves as victims of your actions, they coerce you into acting out of pity, amplifying their control over you. Pity plays thrive when leverage dwindles, serving as a last resort for the manipulator to maintain their influence.

- **Manipulative moralizing:** Ever felt judged for deviating from someone else's moral compass? That's manipulative moralizing at work. It weaponizes guilt, coercing conformity to the manipulator's standards of behavior. By instilling a sense of inadequacy, the manipulator nudges you toward alignment with their ideals or drives you to conceal your true self.

- **Shame attacks:** Intensified moralizations aimed at humiliating and condemning, shame attacks are potent tools wielded by those hungry for power. Through what I term "burning stake shows," individuals tarnish reputations and livelihoods, wielding shame as a weapon of destruction.

- **Sexual manipulation:** Within the realm of sexual dynamics, manipulation takes on nuanced forms. Intrasexual manipulation aims to suppress competition among the same gender, while intersexual manipulation seeks to diminish the dating power of the opposite gender. From cultural norms of sexual loyalty to slut-shaming tactics, these manipulations reinforce power dynamics and control.

- **Manipulation in relationships:** Relationships aren't immune to manipulation; in fact, they can be breeding grounds for it. From trapping partners through esteem erosion and dependency cultivation to acquiring power through emotional manipulation tactics like gaslighting and belittling, manipulators prioritize control over collaboration.

- **Self-manipulation:** Yet, amid external manipulations, we often overlook the most insidious form: self-manipulation. Whether through minimizing, optimism bias, or the sunk-cost fallacy, we deceive ourselves into enduring toxic situations. Recognizing and challenging these internal manipulations is paramount for breaking free from external control.

The most skilled and dangerous manipulators lurk within the shadows of the dark triad: psychopaths, narcissists, and Machiavellian personalities. They traverse the emotional landscape devoid of empathy, manipulating others for their personal gain without a shred of remorse. But how can you tell if you're being trapped in their web of deception?

The signs are subtle yet sneaky, causing great emotional turmoil:

- Has the joy of love morphed into a gnawing fear of loss?

- Do you find your happiness hanging by a thread, entirely dependent on your relationship?

- Are you riding a roller coaster of extreme highs and devastating lows?

- Does the complexity of your relationship leave you feeling like you're tiptoeing through a minefield?

- Have you become the architect of your own misery, unable to pinpoint where it all went wrong?

- Is your relationship a constant obsession, a puzzle you tirelessly try to solve?

- Do you find yourself on shaky ground, never quite sure where you stand with your partner?

If these questions strike a chord, it's time to delve deeper into the manipulation tactics employed by these psychological masters:

- **Intermittent reinforcement:** Like a gambler hooked on sporadic rewards, you're kept on edge by intermittent positive reinforcements.

- **Negative reinforcement:** Punishment or withdrawal lurks around every corner, a deterrent against straying from the manipulator's desires.

- **Intentional meltdown:** Backed into an emotional corner, you're pushed to the brink until you unravel, only to be labeled as "crazy" by the master manipulator.

- **Shifting focus:** When the spotlight turns on the manipulator, they deflect, redirecting attention to your supposed flaws and insecurities.

- **Premature disclosures:** False intimacy is fabricated through carefully curated vulnerability, a tactic designed to ensnare the unsuspecting.

- **Triangulation:** A third party is introduced, real or imagined, to stoke the flames of jealousy and insecurity.

- **Playing victim:** With practiced precision, the manipulator twists the narrative, casting themselves as the innocent party while laying blame at your feet.

- **Indirect insults and abuse:** Your confidence is chipped away, disguised beneath a veneer of advice and subtle jabs.

- **Minimizing:** Actions are dismissed as inconsequential, paving the way for future transgressions.

- **Withdrawal as punishment:** Emotional withdrawal becomes a form of punishment, leaving you isolated and desperate for validation.

- **Invalidation of feelings:** Your emotions are dismissed or mocked, leaving you feeling unseen and unheard.

- **Superficial charm:** Beneath the manipulator's charismatic facade lies an empty void, sucking you into their orbit with promises of grandeur.

- **Intentional forgetting:** Important moments are conveniently erased from memory, leaving you grasping at fragments of truth.

- **Traumatic one-trial learning:** An act of aggression establishes dominance, ensuring compliance through fear and intimidation.

- **Belittling:** Your worth is diminished, your achievements tarnished by sarcasm and ridicule.

- **Putting you on the defensive:** Social dynamics are manipulated to keep you constantly justifying your actions, leaving you on the back foot.

- **Fear:** The specter of abandonment looms large, keeping you tethered to the manipulator's whims with the threat of isolation.

- **Pity play:** Leveraging your empathy, they spin tales of woe to escape accountability, leaving you caught in a cycle of sympathy and manipulation.

- **Justification and rationalization:** Excuses flow freely, obscuring their true intentions behind a veil of reason.

- **Flattery:** Words become weapons, used to disarm and deceive, leaving you vulnerable to their charms.

Trust your instincts, and know that you have the right to question everything.

Real-World Applications

How prevalent is manipulation in our everyday lives? Emotional manipulation and its various strategies can infiltrate any relationship, leaving its victims grappling with its effects. Insights drawn from studies on intimate relationships shed light on the extent of this phenomenon. For instance, one study uncovered that a staggering 40% of women and 32% of men have encountered expressive aggression within relationships. Moreover, a significant portion—41% of women and 43% of men—have experienced coercive manipulation tactics (Karakurt & Silver, 2013).

Delving deeper, research indicates that those with certain personality disorders, such as borderline personality disorder or those exhibiting narcissistic traits, are more prone to engaging in manipulative behaviors. This suggests that manipulation isn't just a random occurrence but can be systematically linked to specific psychological profiles (Mandal & Kocur, 2013).

Considering these statistics, it's evident that manipulation is not an isolated issue but rather a pervasive reality in various social dynamics. Whether it's in personal relationships, professional settings, or even within societal structures, the tactics of manipulation can be insidious and impactful.

Unveiling the Dark Arts of Online Reality

In the shadows of cyberspace, a chilling narrative unfolds—a story of manipulation, deception, and the erosion of truth. The revelations from the Snowden archive shed light on the clandestine maneuvers of intelligence agencies, particularly the Western behemoth GCHQ and its covert unit, the Joint Threat Research Intelligence Group (JTRIG). But what lies beneath the surface of this digital labyrinth? How do these agents infiltrate the internet to manipulate and dismantle reputations (Greenwald, 2014)?

Let's dissect the chilling reality.

Recent exposés have peeled back the layers of deception orchestrated by JTRIG, revealing disturbing tactics aimed at controlling online discourse. Through a series of leaked classified documents, we uncover their playbook: the monitoring of platforms like YouTube and Blogger, the insidious targeting of groups like Anonymous with DDoS attacks, and the use of "honey traps" and viruses as tools of manipulation. But these are just fragments of a much larger picture (Greenwald, 2014).

At the core of JTRIG's mission lie two insidious objectives: to smear targets with false narratives and to engineer social discourse to the advantage of intelligence agencies like GCHQ. Imagine the audacity—fabricating content and attributing it to unsuspecting victims, or posing as victims themselves to tarnish reputations. These are not tactics reserved for enemies of the state but are wielded against ordinary citizens, activists, and dissenters alike.

From leaking confidential information to orchestrating smear campaigns on online forums, the scope of JTRIG's malevolence knows no bounds. It's a chilling reminder that no one is safe from their crosshairs—not even those merely suspected of dissent.

As the veil is lifted on these covert operations, a fundamental question emerges: What moral compass guides these actions? How can any government justify such flagrant abuses of power, operating in the shadows without accountability or oversight? The very fabric of democracy is torn asunder when dissent is stifled and truth becomes a casualty of war.

Armed with this knowledge, we stand at a crossroads—a choice between complicity and resistance. We cannot allow the darkness to engulf us, nor can we turn a blind eye to the erosion of our freedoms. It's time to shine a light on the shadows, to hold accountable those who seek to manipulate, deceive, and destroy.

By understanding their tactics, we empower ourselves to move through the digital landscape with clarity and resilience. Let us forge a path forward—one built on transparency, integrity, and unwavering resolve. As we traverse the digital frontier, let us remain vigilant against the encroaching tide of manipulation.

The revelations from the Snowden archive serve as a stark reminder of the perils that lurk in the digital shadows.

Subliminal Messaging and Persuasion

Unconscious Influence in Communication

Subliminal messaging and persuasion—the veiled mechanisms of unconscious influence lurking beneath the surface of everyday interactions.

Imagine that you're engaged in a conversation, seemingly benign, yet beneath the spoken words lies a web of subtle cues, manipulation, and hidden agendas. This is the realm of unconscious influence in communication, where individuals are swayed without even realizing it.

Let's say you're catching up with an old friend over coffee. The conversation flows smoothly, filled with laughter and reminiscing about shared memories. Yet, unbeknownst to you, subtle cues and manipulative tactics are at play.

As your friend regales you with stories of their recent success, you can't help but feel a twinge of envy creeping in. Without realizing it, your friend's subtle boasting triggers feelings of inadequacy within you, subtly influencing your mood and perception of yourself.

Meanwhile, your friend strategically peppers the conversation with compliments and flattery, subtly stroking your ego and deepening your emotional investment in the interaction. These seemingly innocent gestures serve to subtly manipulate your emotions, fostering a sense of closeness and dependency on your friend.

Unbeknownst to you, your friend's hidden agenda may be to gain your support or validation for their endeavors, subtly steering the conversation toward their own benefit without your conscious awareness. In this scenario, the benign facade of the conversation masks a web of manipulation and hidden agendas, illustrating the power of unconscious influence in communication.

Unconscious influence operates on the premise that our subconscious mind is susceptible to subtle cues, bypassing our conscious awareness. Through carefully crafted language, tone, body language, and even timing, manipulators plant seeds of suggestion that take root in the depths of our psyche.

Consider the power of suggestion in advertising. Ever found yourself craving a particular product after seeing a cleverly crafted commercial? Starving after seeing a McDonald's advert? That's the work of unconscious influence at play. Advertisers leverage subliminal messaging to tap into our desires, fears, and insecurities, subtly nudging us toward their products or ideas.

Using Subliminal Messaging

Picture this: You're sitting in front of your screen, scrolling through your favorite social media platform. Unknown to you, hidden within the flashy images and catchy slogans lies a powerful tool: subliminal messaging. It's a technique employed by those well-versed in the art of psychological manipulation, and it's more pervasive than you might think.

Subliminal messaging operates below the threshold of conscious perception, slipping past your defenses and planting seeds of influence directly into your subconscious mind. It's subtle, insidious, and incredibly effective. But how does it work?

Imagine a movie theater, where frames flicker by at a rate too rapid for your conscious mind to register. Among these frames are brief images or words, strategically placed to evoke certain emotions or associations. You may not consciously notice them, but rest assured, your subconscious mind does.

In the world of advertising, subliminal messaging is a common tactic used to sway consumer behavior. Whether it's the faint image of a brand logo hidden in a print ad or the subtle whisper of a product name in a television commercial, advertisers leverage subliminal cues to influence your purchasing decisions without you even realizing it.

But subliminal messaging isn't limited to marketing. It can be found in various forms of media, from political campaigns to propaganda efforts. The goal remains the same: to shape your thoughts, beliefs, and behaviors in subtle yet powerful ways.

So, how can you protect yourself from such manipulation? The key lies in awareness and vigilance. By educating yourself about the techniques of subliminal messaging and remaining mindful of the media you consume, you can begin to recognize and resist its influence.

Here are some practical strategies to shield yourself from subliminal messaging:

- **Stay vigilant:** Pay attention to the content you're exposed to and question the motives behind it. Is there an underlying agenda? Are you being subtly manipulated?

- **Limit exposure:** Be mindful of the media you consume and the environments you expose yourself to. If you suspect subliminal messaging is at play, consider distancing yourself from those sources.

- **Critical thinking:** Train yourself to think critically about the information presented to you. Don't take things at face value— dig deeper and question the underlying messages.

- **Mindfulness:** Practice mindfulness techniques to strengthen your awareness of your own thoughts and feelings. By staying grounded in the present moment, you can better resist external influences.

- **Seek alternative sources:** Diversify your media intake and seek out alternative sources of information. Exposing yourself to a range of perspectives can help counteract the effects of subliminal messaging.

Stay vigilant, stay informed, and remember: The power lies within you. Be a persuasive communicator.

Ethical Considerations in Subliminal Messaging

First, consider the issue of consent. Subliminal messages operate beneath the threshold of conscious perception, meaning people may be manipulated without their explicit consent or awareness. This raises significant ethical concerns regarding autonomy and personal agency. How can we justify manipulating someone's thoughts or actions without their informed consent? It's a violation of basic ethical principles and undermines the fundamental right of that person to make their own choices.

Furthermore, there's the question of intentionality. Are subliminal messages being used for the greater good, or are they being wielded as a weapon of manipulation? In many cases, the latter holds true, as people or entities seek to exploit others for personal gain or control. This blatant disregard for the well-being of others is not only unethical but also morally reprehensible. We must scrutinize the motives behind the use of subliminal messaging and hold accountable those who seek to use it for nefarious purposes.

Another crucial ethical consideration is the potential for harm. Subliminal messages can have profound effects on people, shaping their beliefs, attitudes, and behaviors without their conscious awareness. This raises concerns about the unintended consequences of such manipulation. What if the messages instill harmful ideologies or encourage destructive behaviors? The psychological damage inflicted can be long-lasting and devastating.

In light of these ethical considerations, it's imperative to establish safeguards and regulations governing the use of subliminal messaging. Transparency and accountability are key. People should be made aware of any attempts to influence them subliminally, and mechanisms should be in place to ensure that such tactics are used responsibly and ethically.

We must also empower ourselves with knowledge and awareness to recognize and resist attempts at subliminal manipulation. By educating ourselves about the techniques employed in dark psychology, we can become more resilient to their effects and protect ourselves from undue influence. Critical thinking and skepticism are our greatest allies in the battle against psychological warfare.

Manipulative Influence in Various Aspects of Life

Workplace Dynamics

The workplace is a breeding ground for manipulative influence. From subtle power plays to overt control tactics, dark psychology thrives in the professional arena—often under the guise of ambition and competition. Let's explore the insidious ways manipulative dynamics manifest in the workplace and how to shield yourself from their grasp:

- **Office politics:** In every workplace, there exists an undercurrent of office politics. It's the place where alliances are formed and power is wielded behind closed doors. Manipulators thrive in this environment, using charm, manipulation, and strategic maneuvering to advance their agendas. They may employ tactics like spreading rumors, backstabbing, or sabotaging colleagues to climb the corporate ladder.

  - **Actionable strategy:** Stay vigilant and build genuine relationships based on trust and mutual respect. Keep your focus on your work and maintain professional boundaries. Document important interactions and confront manipulative behavior assertively when necessary.

- **Hierarchical manipulation:** Hierarchies inherently breed power differentials, creating fertile ground for manipulation. Superiors may exert control through micromanagement, favoritism, or exploiting their authority. Subordinates may resort to flattery, manipulation, or even manipulation of information to curry favor or evade accountability.

  - **Actionable strategy:** Understand your rights and responsibilities within the organizational structure. Advocate for yourself professionally and seek mentorship from ethical leaders who prioritize fairness and transparency. Document instances of abuse of power and escalate concerns through appropriate channels.

- **Cultivating resilience:** Ultimately, the key to combating manipulative influence in the workplace lies in cultivating resilience and self-awareness. By understanding the tactics employed by manipulators and strengthening your psychological defenses, you can navigate challenging dynamics with confidence and integrity.

  - **Actionable strategy:** Invest in your personal and professional development, honing skills like assertiveness, critical thinking, and conflict resolution. Cultivate a strong support network of trusted colleagues, mentors, or therapists who can provide guidance and validation. Remember, you have the power to protect yourself and thrive in any professional environment.

In the battleground of the workplace, knowledge is your friend against manipulative influence. Do your best to understand the subtle nuances of dark psychology, and implement proactive strategies so you can safeguard your mental and emotional well-being while forging a path to success on your own terms.

Social and Personal Relationships

From subtle maneuvers to overt coercion, manipulative influence can permeate your social and personal relationships. Let's explore its manifestations across different domains:

- **Social dynamics:** In the social arena, manipulation can manifest in numerous ways. Whether it's the friend who subtly undermines your confidence to bolster their own ego or the colleague who spreads rumors to sabotage your reputation, manipulation thrives amid social dynamics. Ask yourself: Have you ever felt uneasy around certain individuals, sensing an underlying agenda or feeling emotionally drained after interactions? These could be signs of manipulative influence at play.

- **Personal relationships:** Within intimate relationships, manipulation can be particularly insidious. It might take the form of gaslighting, or it could manifest as emotional blackmail. Reflect on your own relationships: Do you feel respected and valued, or do you find yourself constantly second-guessing your own feelings and choices? Recognizing these dynamics is vital when reclaiming your power.

- **Media and advertising:** Beyond personal interactions, manipulative influence permeates the media landscape. From sensationalist headlines designed to provoke emotional reactions to targeted advertising that exploits psychological vulnerabilities, the media often serves as a battleground for manipulation. Ask yourself: How do you consume information? Are you critically evaluating sources and content, or are you being swayed by subtle persuasion techniques? Developing media literacy is crucial in safeguarding against manipulation in this digital age.

In each of these aspects of life, manipulation exerts its influence, shaping perceptions, decisions, and behaviors. Remember, you have the power to unpack the complexities of human interaction with clarity, resilience, and self-assurance.

Interactive Element: The Big Picture

Alright, let's zoom back out and look at the big picture. Imagine navigating life's minefields, unaware of manipulative tactics. But with knowledge, you can become impervious to their strategies. This framework serves as your shield against psychological warfare.

Returning to the A.M.E.L.I.O.R.A.T.E. framework, we revisit the fourth stage, "Leading covert techniques in dark psychology." We have reviewed how to recognize the signs and subtle cues, how to anchor yourself in the present moment, discerning reality from manipulation, and how to reclaim control over your thoughts and actions. Listen to your gut instinct, guiding you toward truth. See things objectively, separating fact from fiction. Bounce back stronger than before. Set clear boundaries and stand up for yourself. Press forward, undeterred by challenges. Understand the motivations behind manipulation, fostering connection and compassion.

Are you ready to embark on this journey of self-discovery and empowerment?

As we conclude this chapter, it's crucial to recognize the profound impact such knowledge can have on safeguarding our mental and emotional well-being. By shedding light on the insidious tactics employed by manipulators, we arm ourselves with a potent shield against their schemes.

In the following chapter, we'll explore the next stage of the framework, "Introducing self-protection." Are you ready to learn how to protect yourself?

Chapter 5:

Introducing Self-Protection

In the hands of a skilled manipulator, words become weapons and silence becomes an ally. –Machiavelli

As we delve deeper into the fifth phase of the A.M.E.L.I.O.R.A.T.E. framework, our focus sharpens onto self-protection—the shield against psychological onslaughts that threaten our autonomy and well-being. Here, we confront the uncomfortable reality that our minds are not impervious to manipulation; rather, they are vulnerable to the cunning tactics employed by individuals with malicious intent.

But fear not, for knowledge is our greatest armor, and understanding the intricate mechanisms of dark psychology is the first step toward fortification. Through a lens of insight and clarity, we shall unravel the deceptive tactics employed by manipulators and cultivate a steadfast resilience against their influence.

The journey toward self-protection is not merely about defense; it is a transformative process that empowers us to navigate the complexities of human interaction with wisdom and discernment. By the journey's end, you will emerge equipped with the tools to recognize, counter, and transcend the dark forces that seek to ensnare your mind.

But remember, empowerment does not grant license for aggression. As we embark on this path, let us uphold the principles of ethical conduct and empathy. Our aim is not to retaliate in kind but to safeguard our mental sovereignty while fostering a culture of mutual respect and understanding.

Are you ready to embark on this journey of self-protection? Prepare to arm yourself with knowledge, resilience, and unwavering resolve as we navigate the treacherous waters of dark psychology, emerging stronger and more enlightened than before. Together, let us reclaim our minds and forge a future free from the shackles of manipulation.

What Manipulation Looks Like in Ourselves

We have discovered that manipulation is a tactic to make someone do what you want. It's like trying to trick them into acting a certain way, such as giving you something or doing something for you, without being direct about it. Instead, you try to persuade them without their knowledge.

Ken Page, LCSW, a therapist and relationship expert, believes that everyone can be manipulative from time to time, often without even realizing it. He states, "We are all human, and all of us manipulate because it's a human defense mechanism" (Regan, 2023).

Are you ready to face the mirror of your own mind? Manipulation, that subtle dance of influence, is a skill we all wield to some extent. From the gentle nudge to the outright coercion, we've all been players in this psychological game. But understanding our own manipulative tendencies isn't just about self-reflection; it's about safeguarding our relationships and our integrity.

It's time to scrutinize our own behaviors, recognize the signs of manipulation within ourselves, and pave the way to a more authentic interaction with the world.

What does manipulation look like in the mirror of self-awareness? It's that sly maneuver to bend someone's will to our desires without their conscious realization. Yet, before we cast judgment upon others, let's turn the spotlight inward. Manipulation isn't a trait reserved for the conniving few; it's a shadow lurking within us all. We manipulate as a reflex born from our humanity.

But what behaviors should we watch out for in the theater of our own minds?

Ask yourself the following:

- Does your kindness, once pure, now harbor ulterior motives— a barter for future favors?

- Do you impose your fears on others, creating false fears?

- Do you spread lies like poison if things don't go your way?

- Is guilt your weapon to get someone to say yes?

- Do you make promises to get others to do what you want or need and then not follow through?

- Do you struggle to express your true needs clearly, often hiding them behind half-truths?

- Will you go to great lengths to get what you want, bending reality to your desires with expert skill?

If you spot manipulative behavior in yourself, there is hope. Being aware helps us see through deception. It shows us our flaws and points us toward being genuine.

How can we stop this cycle of manipulation? It starts with being brutally honest, sharing our true intentions without tricks or deceit. It means being open about our vulnerabilities, expressing our wants and fears honestly. It's about accepting our truths, even when they're difficult or inconvenient.

Self-awareness is where you need to begin. Embrace it, nurture it, and wield it as a shield against the darkness of manipulation. This is where your power lies to forge authentic connections and reclaim your humanity.

Why Do We Become Manipulative?

So, how does one become manipulative? It's a question that looks deep into the intricate layers of human psychology. According to specialists, it often stems from a deep-seated belief that if you were to genuinely ask for what you want and need, the response would inevitably be a resounding "no." This mindset can take root from unmet needs during your upbringing, possibly exacerbated by witnessing manipulation within your own family dynamic (Regan, 2023).

Manipulation begins to act as a shield against confronting past traumas. The more profound the trauma, the more challenging it becomes to confront and process it without resorting to manipulation or succumbing to post-traumatic stress responses.

While some personalities, like sociopaths and narcissists, seem inherently inclined to manipulation, for most, it's a spectrum. Trauma often acts as fertile ground for manipulative tendencies to flourish.

Digging beneath the surface to uncover the pain that drives this behavior is key. From there, it's about learning to care for yourself within that pain and interact from a place of emotional health.

Undoing hardwired manipulative patterns isn't easy—it requires rewiring deeply ingrained circuits. Being open with those closest to you, inviting them to gently call out manipulative behaviors when they arise, can be helpful.

Mindfulness becomes your ally in this healing path. Constantly question your intentions in your interactions: What are you truly trying to achieve here? Are you being forthright and honest? These inquiries serve as guideposts toward more authentic communication.

With introspection, healing, and a commitment to genuine connection, you can transcend manipulation, fulfilling your needs with integrity and honesty. These tools will help you more effectively manage your life; unintentionally employing dark psychology is not as mindful and beneficial as using it skillfully.

Developing a Strong Sense of Self-Awareness

To survive the dangerous waters of dark psychology, you must first anchor yourself firmly in the harbor of self-understanding. Let's explore the power of developing a strong sense of self-awareness through mindfulness and self-reflection, forging a shield against manipulation.

Mindfulness and Self-Reflection

You stand in the midst of a storm, surrounded by swirling doubts, fears, and hidden agendas. In this tempest, clarity becomes elusive and your sense of self wavers like a ship on rough seas.

Now, imagine if you possessed a lantern of self-awareness, lighting the shadows and revealing the hidden currents of manipulation. This is the essence of mindfulness and self-reflection.

Mindfulness fosters a heightened awareness of the present moment, sharpening your perception like a finely honed blade. It allows you to observe thoughts, emotions, and external influences without judgment, fostering a deep understanding of your own psyche.

Self-reflection, on the other hand, is the mirror that reflects your inner landscape, enabling you to dissect experiences, beliefs, and behaviors with precision.

When you embrace mindfulness and self-reflection, you surpass the depths of unconscious influence, emerging as the architect of your own reality. No longer a pawn or player in the game of manipulation, you become a vigilant guardian of your mental fortress.

How to Engage With Mindfulness and Self-Reflection

Here are actionable steps to integrate mindfulness and self-reflection into your daily life, strengthening your defenses against dark psychology:

- **Anchor yourself in the present:** Begin each day with a mindfulness ritual. Notice the ebb and flow of your thoughts and emotions without becoming entangled in their web. Give the following a try:

  - **Nature immersion:** Take a mindful walk in nature, focusing on the sights, sounds, and sensations around you. Tune into the rustle of leaves, the chirping of birds, and the gentle caress of the breeze. Engage your senses fully, allowing the natural world to envelop you in its embrace.

  - **Tea ceremony:** Create a sacred space for a tea ceremony, where each step—from boiling water to steeping tea leaves—is performed with mindful intention. Notice the aroma rising from the cup, the warmth spreading through your body, and the flavors dancing on your palate. Savor each sip as if it were a sip of serenity.

  - **Sound bath:** Immerse yourself in the healing vibrations of a sound bath, whether it's through singing bowls, gongs, other musical instruments, or an app. Lie down in a comfortable position, close your eyes, and surrender to the waves of sound washing over you. Allow the vibrations to penetrate every cell of your being, releasing tension and restoring harmony.

- ○ **Digital detox:** Dedicate a period of time each day to disconnecting from digital distractions and immersing yourself fully in the present moment. Turn off your devices, step away from screens, and engage in activities that nourish your mind, body, and soul—try reading a book, taking a leisurely stroll, or simply basking in solitude.

- **Question everything:** Adopt a stance of curiosity and inquiry toward your own thoughts, beliefs, and actions. When confronted with a persuasive argument or a subtle manipulation attempt, pause and interrogate your inner motives. Ask yourself: What biases or vulnerabilities are you overlooking? How does this align with your values and goals?

- **Journal your journey:** Keep a reflective journal as your trusted confidant and ally. Dedicate time each day to pouring your thoughts onto the page, dissecting experiences and unraveling the threads of influence. Explore patterns, triggers, and blind spots with ruthless honesty, shedding light on the shadows of your subconscious.

- **Seek feedback:** Surround yourself with trusted allies who serve as mirrors for your growth. Solicit feedback from friends, mentors, or therapists, inviting their insights into your blind spots and areas for improvement. Embrace constructive criticism as a catalyst for growth rather than a blow to your ego.

- **Practice discernment:** Develop a discerning eye toward the tactics of manipulation and gaslighting. Continue to educate yourself on the principles of dark psychology, studying the subtle cues and strategies employed by manipulators.

Nurturing Emotional Intelligence

Emotional intelligence, or EQ, isn't solely about defense—it's a catalyst for positive engagement even within the intricate landscape of dark psychology. Let's explore how you can harness your emotional intelligence not just to protect yourself but to positively influence psychological dynamics:

- **Self-awareness:** Acknowledge that your initial judgments can be portals for understanding and connection. When you consciously refine your ability to perceive others beyond surface impressions, you open doors to empathy and genuine understanding. Use this skill to forge deeper connections, recognizing the humanity in others and fostering trust and collaboration.

- **Self-regulation:** Understand that every reaction is an opportunity for growth and impact. Instead of succumbing to impulsive responses, foster mindful control over your emotions and behaviors. Channel your reactions toward constructive outcomes, growing harmony and resilience in your relationships. By mastering self-regulation, you cultivate an environment of mutual respect and cooperation.

- **Motivation:** Recognize that motivation is the engine driving positive change and growth. Tap into your intrinsic desires and values, using them to propel yourself and others toward shared goals. Whether it's inspiring innovation, fostering teamwork, or promoting personal development, align your actions with noble intentions to uplift and empower those around you.

- **Empathy:** Embrace empathy as a cornerstone of compassionate leadership and understanding. Develop the ability to deeply connect with others, intuitively sensing their emotions and perspectives. Use this insight to support and uplift others, offering a listening ear and a compassionate heart.

By gaining empathy-driven interactions, you foster a culture of inclusivity and belonging, enriching both personal and professional relationships.

- **Social skills:** Recognize that social interactions are opportunities for positive impact and growth. Master the art of effective communication, collaboration, and conflict resolution, using them to build bridges and foster understanding. Treat every interaction as a chance to uplift and empower others, fostering a culture of kindness, respect, and mutual support.

In essence, emotional intelligence is a force for positive transformation, even within the world of dark psychology. When you take the steps to harness these skills with integrity and empathy, you can foster authentic connections and nurture a culture of mutual respect and understanding.

Building Resilience Against Psychological Manipulation

In the complex landscape of psychological manipulation, resilience acts as a shield against the subtle and often deceptive tactics employed by manipulators. But what exactly does resilience entail, and how does it safeguard us from the harmful effects of gaslighting and dark psychology?

Think of resilience as a mighty oak tree standing tall in the face of a raging storm. It's not merely about surviving the tempest but flourishing in its midst, displaying the inner fortitude and emotional stability to endure turbulent times.

So, how does this mental and emotional resilience protect us from falling prey to manipulative schemes?

Let's consider a relatable scenario. Say you're in a relationship where your partner consistently undermines your self-confidence, subtly twisting your perceptions until you doubt your own worth. But if you've built resilience, you're less likely to succumb to these tactics. You know your own value, you trust your instincts, and you refuse to let anyone else define your truth.

Resilience also sharpens our critical thinking skills, allowing us to see through manipulative tactics and question the narratives presented to us. For instance, imagine you're pitched a too-good-to-be-true investment opportunity by a persuasive salesperson. Instead of being swayed by their charisma, resilience prompts you to scrutinize the proposal, weigh the risks, and make an informed decision based on facts rather than emotions.

Furthermore, resilience equips us with emotional intelligence—the ability to recognize and manage our own emotions effectively. Let's say you encounter a colleague who constantly belittles your contributions, attempting to provoke a reaction. With resilience, you remain composed, refusing to give them the satisfaction of seeing you upset. You understand that their behavior reflects their own insecurities, and you choose not to let it affect your self-esteem.

So, how can we strengthen our mental and emotional resilience to safeguard ourselves against manipulation?

Again, rely heavily on building self-awareness. Reflect on your values, strengths, and vulnerabilities. Knowing yourself empowers you to set boundaries and recognize when those boundaries are being tested.

Next, hone your critical thinking skills. Question information presented to you, especially if it seems too good to be true. Look for evidence, seek multiple perspectives, and trust your intuition.

Additionally, practice emotional regulation techniques such as deep breathing or mindfulness meditation. These tools help you stay grounded in moments of stress or conflict, preventing manipulators from exploiting your emotions.

Finally, surround yourself with supportive friends, family, or mentors who uplift and validate you. Having a strong support network bolsters your resilience and provides perspective when faced with challenging situations.

Strengthening Resilience

Do you find yourself bouncing back from setbacks or crumbling under pressure? Resilience isn't just about enduring tough times; it's about thriving in spite of them. When challenges arise, do you have the inner fortitude to persevere?

Resilience gives you the power to get through life when it gets messy without losing sight of your strength and purpose. It's the ability to move through adversity while maintaining your physical and psychological well-being. Without resilience, you might find yourself immobilized by problems, feeling like a helpless victim trapped in a cycle of negativity or manipulation.

But resilience is not innate; it's a skill that can be built and grown. With resilience, you can confront challenges head-on, refusing to be defeated by psychological warfare. It won't magically erase your problems, but it will equip you with the mindset and tools to overcome them.

Let's look at some ways to help sharpen your resilience:

- **Cultivate connections:** We have covered isolation and how those trying to manipulate you may try to keep you from those who can support you. Do your best to surround yourself with a supportive network of friends and family. Strong relationships provide a safety net during dark times, offering comfort, guidance, and encouragement.

- **Infuse meaning into each day:** When you're in the thick of it, it can be truly difficult to be grateful. But it does help. Find purpose in your daily activities. Set small, achievable goals for yourself that align with your values and aspirations, giving you a sense of accomplishment and direction. When you infuse meaning into your life, you'll approach it with renewed spirit and determination.

- **Reflect on past triumphs:** Look back on past challenges and how you overcame them. Reflecting on your resilience in hindsight can illuminate patterns of behavior and coping strategies that proved effective. Consider journaling about your experiences to gain insight into your resilience journey and inform future actions.

- **Foster hope:** Adopt optimism and maintain a forward-thinking mindset. While you can't change the past, you can shape the future with a hopeful outlook. Open yourself to change, embracing new opportunities with optimism and resilience.

- **Prioritize self-care:** Take care of your physical, emotional, and mental well-being. Choose activities that bring you joy and fulfillment, incorporating exercise, adequate sleep, and healthy habits into your routine.

- **Take action:** Don't passively accept adversity; take proactive steps to address your challenges. Identify the necessary actions, formulate a plan, and take decisive steps toward resolution. Though recovery may take time, progress is achievable through consistent effort and determination.

If you find yourself struggling or unsure of where to begin, don't hesitate to seek guidance from a mental health professional. With support and dedication, you can nurture resilience and enhance your mental well-being, empowering yourself to thrive when life gets tough.

Developing Cognitive Defenses

Meet Heather and Michelle.

In the dynamic streets of New York City, two companions, Heather and Michelle, shared a living space. Both were flourishing in their respective careers—Heather, an up-and-coming artist, and Michelle, a determined corporate professional. Despite their differing paths, their bond was strong, fueled by mutual respect for each other's aspirations.

Yet, as time elapsed, Heather began noticing a shift in Michelle's demeanor. Subtle jabs at Heather's accomplishments crept into their conversations, insinuating that her artistry paled in significance compared to Michelle's corporate endeavors. Heather couldn't shake off the growing sense of inadequacy.

When Heather received an invitation to showcase her artwork at a prestigious gallery, it was a moment of pure elation. Eager to share her joy, she turned to Michelle. But instead of celebrating, Michelle's response was dismissive, her words dripping with indifference. "Is that really such a big deal in your world?" she remarked. Heather felt a sting of hurt but brushed it aside, attributing it to Michelle's possible stress.

However, Michelle didn't stop there. She weaponized Heather's insecurities, exploiting every hint of self-doubt. Each time Heather expressed uncertainty about her work, Michelle amplified her anxieties. "Maybe you're right; perhaps your art isn't gallery-worthy," she'd say, driving Heather deeper into uncertainty.

Michelle was also skilled in the art of gaslighting. When Heather confronted her about the demeaning comments, Michelle vehemently denied them, leaving Heather questioning her own recollection. "You must be mistaken; I would never say such things. You know I'm your biggest supporter," Michelle argued.

With each passing day, Heather felt her anxiety escalate. Trusting Michelle had always been a given, and the notion of manipulation seemed implausible. Yet, a nagging feeling persisted.

One evening, their mutual friend Daniel paid a visit. A seasoned psychologist, he noticed the tension between Heather and Michelle. Heather confided in Daniel, laying bare her struggles with Michelle's behavior.

After hearing Heather's story, Daniel suggested that Michelle might be manipulating her, exploiting her insecurities to undermine her confidence. He highlighted the gaslighting tactics, emotional coercion, and consistent undermining as telltale signs of psychological manipulation.

Initially resistant, Heather began to see the patterns more clearly. With Daniel's guidance, she mustered the courage to confront Michelle, armed with her awareness of gaslighting and denial. When Michelle refuted her actions, Heather stood her ground, articulating her feelings with unwavering conviction.

Michelle, caught off guard by Heather's newfound assertiveness, eventually confessed to feeling threatened by Heather's success. She apologized for her behavior, acknowledging the harm she had caused. Heather made the decision to distance herself from Michelle, prioritizing her mental well-being and focusing on her flourishing art career, which saw tremendous success.

This narrative underscores how psychological manipulation can infiltrate even the closest of bonds, breeding self-doubt and confusion. It underscores the significance of recognizing these tactics, seeking support, asserting boundaries, and prioritizing one's mental health.

Defense Mechanisms Utilized to Protect Ourselves

Defense mechanisms are automatic responses in the mind that help protect people from anxious feelings, threats to how they view themselves, and things they prefer not to acknowledge or deal with (Cramer, 2015).

Cognitive defenses are a crucial aspect in shielding ourselves against the insidious tactics of psychological manipulation. Sigmund Freud laid the groundwork for understanding these defenses, seeing them as vital barriers safeguarding our conscious mind from the conflicting forces of our primal instincts and societal norms. This concept of "mental homeostasis" is pivotal in maintaining our psychological equilibrium amid the chaos of manipulation (Waqas et al., 2015).

Building upon Freud's work, his daughter, Anna Freud, elaborated on these defenses, identifying 10 distinct mechanisms employed by the ego (Cherry, 2023a). As you explore these mechanisms, it's imperative that you discern whether any resonate with your own experiences. Are you familiar with the strategies your mind may instinctively employ to protect itself?

Defense mechanism	Description	Example
Regression	Returning to earlier habits or behaviors.	Holding onto a soft blanket when you are anxious, reminiscent of your childhood days.
Intellectualization	Thinking of stressors clinically.	The loss of a loved one and avoiding grief by overworking.
Reaction formation	Replacing an unwanted impulse with its opposite.	Being devastated over a job loss but acting happy to others.
Rationalization	Justifying an unacceptable feeling or behavior with logic.	Losing out on a dream job and saying it was for the best because you wouldn't have liked the job anyway.
Sublimation	Converting inappropriate urges	Being mad with your friend but talking it

	into more acceptable forms.	out instead of fighting.
Displacement	Taking strong emotions out on others.	Being frustrated at your coworker but taking it out on your partner instead.
Repression	Unknowingly blocking unpleasant information from your aware mind.	Being neglected as a child but not blocking the abuse.
Suppression	Consciously avoiding unpleasant information.	Being abused by your partner but living your life and ignoring the abuse.
Projection	Projecting your own undesirable emotions or characteristics onto others.	Flirting with someone other than your spouse, then being anxious that your spouse is the one cheating.
Denial	Denying that something exists.	Being the victim of a violent crime, but denying it ever happened.

An Inner Meter on Manipulation

Are you exhausted because you feel you have no say in your life, as if someone else is calling all the shots? It's time to reclaim your power and develop your cognitive defenses against manipulation. But how can you even begin to recognize when you're being manipulated? It starts with tuning in to your inner signals.

What happens when you're in a situation and something just doesn't feel right? Maybe you're feeling uneasy, off-balance, or disconnected. These are red flags waving, signaling that you might be under someone else's influence. Pay attention to those nagging feelings of discomfort—they're your body's way of alerting you to potential manipulation.

Notice when your values don't align with the actions and words of those around you. When you're left feeling drained after interactions, it could be a sign that someone is sapping your energy, leaving you depleted. And be wary of ego-driven agendas that hijack your thoughts and actions, steering you away from your authentic self.

Take a moment to reflect: Have you ever found yourself acting in a way that doesn't feel like "you"? Do you ever walk away from a situation wondering, *Who am I anymore?* That's your inner meter on manipulation ringing loud and clear. Trust it. And don't hesitate to extend your awareness to those closest to you—sometimes, they need a gentle nudge to see through the manipulation too.

Now, let's talk about response. When your inner alarm goes off, resist the urge to react impulsively. Instead, take a step back and assess the situation. Remember, you always have the power to set boundaries and make choices that align with your true self. Sometimes, the most powerful action is simply refusing to play along.

It's all about rewriting the script. Visualize yourself navigating those tricky situations with grace and strength. Take that relative, for instance, who never hesitates to use guilt to insist you visit more often. Ask yourself how you could better handle this situation. Start by owning your time and energy. It is valuable and you are worthy, no explanation needed. Next, tell this relative when you're available to visit without offering up reasons. Take back that power while still remaining respectful. The truth is that we all have choices, and it's important to know and honor them. The non-manipulated life belongs to you, unless you play small. You call the shots in your life.

And remember, you're not a helpless victim of circumstances. Regardless of what life throws your way, you have the power to choose your attitude and frame your experiences.

Interactive Element: The Big Picture

Now, let's zoom out and see the bigger picture through the lens of the A.M.E.L.I.O.R.A.T.E. framework.

At this point, we've journeyed through the fifth stage of the framework, "Introducing self-protection." But why is this understanding essential? It's not merely academic; it's about reclaiming power and freedom in your life.

Think about it. How many times have you felt bewildered by someone's actions, questioning your own sanity or perception of reality? Gaslighting thrives on this confusion, weakening your sense of self and leaving you vulnerable to manipulation.

But armed with this continuous knowledge, you become immune to these tactics. You recognize the subtle signs of manipulation, from covert mind games to outright deception. You understand the psychological mechanisms at play, allowing you to maintain clarity and assertiveness in the face of manipulation.

It's about reclaiming your power, protecting your mental well-being, and forging authentic connections based on trust and integrity. So, as you navigate the complexities of human behavior, remember this framework as your path to a brighter, more resilient future.

In conclusion, safeguarding your mental and emotional well-being is mandatory during this phase. You've equipped yourself with the knowledge to recognize the subtle signs of manipulation, thereby reclaiming control over your own narrative.

On this road to self-protection, action is paramount. Remember to trust your instincts, cultivate self-awareness, and establish firm boundaries.

As we move forward, the next chapter will move deeper into the overtures of gaslighting. Prepare to explore the intricate web of lies and distortions designed to erode your sense of reality. Learn how to fortify your mind against these gaslighting tactics and emerge stronger than ever before.

Chapter 6:

Overtures of Gaslighting

The true master of manipulation can control others without them even realizing it. –
Robert Cialdini

Welcome to the sixth phase of the A.M.E.L.I.O.R.A.T.E. framework: "Overtures of gaslighting." Prepare to unravel psychological manipulation, where understanding is the key to empowerment.

Gaslighting is not merely a plot device but a real and potent weapon used in psychological warfare. It's a subtle and cunning form of manipulation that can leave even the most resilient of us questioning our entire world, our entire being.

In this chapter, we'll strip away the veil of deception and reveal the mechanics behind gaslighting. We'll explore the various techniques used by gaslighters to cast doubt and confusion in their targets' minds. From outright denial of reality to subtle undermining of confidence, gaslighting takes many forms, each more evil than the last.

This chapter will give you the knowledge needed to recognize gaslighting when it rears its ugly head and to respond with clarity and confidence. You'll learn to trust your instincts, validate your experiences, and reclaim control over your own narrative.

So, are you ready to journey into the shadows of the mind and confront the specter of gaslighting head-on?

Understanding Gaslighting and Its Impact

Gaslighting, the psychological manipulation tactic, has surged into our collective consciousness, becoming a defining term of our era. Merriam-Webster's "Word of the Year" in 2022, it witnessed a staggering 1,740% spike in lookups during this time (*Word of the Year*, 2023). But beyond its lexical definition lies a sinister place of mental exploitation.

At its core, gaslighting embodies the deliberate distortion of reality to serve the manipulator's agenda. Imagine being told your perceptions are flawed, your emotions exaggerated, your very grasp on reality shaky. This is gaslighting in action. It's not just a matter of misleading; it's a calculated assault on your psyche.

Traditionally, gaslighting evoked extreme scenarios leading to mental illness or institutionalization. However, its scope has broadened, infiltrating various facets of life. Contrary to popular belief, it's not confined to romantic relationships or gender stereotypes. It thrives in workplaces, families, and even professional settings, morphing into a pervasive force of psychological coercion.

What makes gaslighting so deceptive is its subtlety. It thrives in the shadows, cloaked in plausible deniability. Manipulators wield phrases like weapons, undermining your reality, shifting blame, and casting doubt with precision.

Here's a closer look at some of these phrases (Sweeney & Dolgoff, 2024):

- **"I really think you need to calm down."**

   When someone tells you to calm down in response to your passionate expression of feelings, they're trivializing your emotions and dismissing your valid concerns. This can leave you feeling invalidated and doubting yourself.

- **"I'm pretty sure you dreamt that?"**

This phrase aims to undermine your memory and make you question your own recollection of events. It's a tactic used to evade accountability and manipulate you into doubting yourself.

- **"I'm very concerned—you're all over the place."**

While concern for your well-being is valid, this phrase can be weaponized to undermine your confidence and control your behavior. Be cautious of individuals who use alleged concern as a guise for manipulation.

- **"I'm apologize if you're upset, but..."**

This pseudo-apology deflects responsibility and places the blame on you for your emotions. Don't accept apologies that come with strings attached or that attempt to invalidate your feelings.

- **"I don't understand why you're doing this to me."**

This tactic flips the script, portraying the gaslighter as the victim and inducing feelings of guilt and self-doubt in you. Stay grounded in your truth and recognize when someone is attempting to manipulate your emotions.

- **"You know in your heart that I would never hurt you."**

Gaslighters may use this phrase to minimize their harmful actions and elicit sympathy from you. Don't let empty promises or excuses cloud your judgment.

- **"Stop being so emotional all the time."**

This dismissive remark aims to invalidate your feelings and portray emotional expression as a weakness. Emotions are valid and essential aspects of human experience.

- **"Are you complaining again? You think your life is so hard."**

Sarcasm and trivialization are often employed to undermine your struggles and minimize your experiences. Recognize when someone is attempting to invalidate your feelings, and assert your right to express yourself without judgment.

- **"You're confused—I never agreed to that."**

Denial and rewriting history are common tactics used by gaslighters to distort reality and manipulate your perception of events. Trust in your own memory.

- **"You're remembering it wrong."**

Gaslighters may outright deny or distort your version of events to undermine your credibility and control your narrative. Trust in your truth and stand firm in your convictions.

Psychological and Emotional Consequences

Gaslighting is not merely a tool of manipulation; it's a psychological assault on your reality, leaving profound scars on your psyche. Your perceptions are constantly undermined, your memories distorted, and your sanity questioned. The emotional fallout is immense, leading to a profound sense of confusion, self-doubt, and even identity crisis.

Imagine living in a world where you can't trust your own thoughts and feelings. Gaslighting shatters your confidence in your own reality, leaving you feeling lost and vulnerable. You begin to question everything about yourself, from your judgments to your beliefs, creating a profound sense of inner turmoil.

When someone systematically undermines your reality, it's easy to start believing that you're inherently flawed or incompetent. You become hypervigilant, constantly second-guessing yourself and seeking validation from others. Your once-strong sense of self begins to crumble under the weight of constant manipulation.

Moreover, gaslighting can lead to profound feelings of isolation and loneliness. When you're constantly being gaslit, it's hard to trust anyone, even those closest to you. You may withdraw from relationships out of fear of being betrayed or manipulated again, further deepening your sense of isolation.

The emotional consequences of gaslighting can be long-lasting and far-reaching. Many survivors report experiencing symptoms of anxiety, depression, and even post-traumatic stress disorder (PTSD). The constant psychological battling takes a toll on your mental health, leaving you feeling emotionally exhausted and drained.

Recognizing Signs of Gaslighting in Relationships

Recognizing signs of gaslighting is crucial for preserving your mental well-being and protecting yourself from its damaging effects. Let's start by reviewing common behavioral indicators that may signal gaslighting in a relationship:

- **Constant denial and contradiction:** Gaslighters habitually deny things they've said or done, even when confronted with evidence. They'll twist facts and contradict themselves to make you doubt your own memory and perception.

- **Blatant lies and exaggerations:** They fabricate stories or exaggerate facts to manipulate your understanding of events. By distorting reality, they aim to maintain control over your thoughts and actions.

- **Selective amnesia:** Gaslighters conveniently "forget" important conversations or agreements, leaving you feeling confused and doubting your own recollection of events. This selective memory serves their agenda of power and control.

- **Exploiting what you love:** Gaslighters use this manipulative strategy to cause you to doubt people and things that are close to you. For instance, if someone cherishes their career, the gaslighter will pinpoint faults in it. Similarly, if the target has children, the gaslighter might insinuate that person should not have become a parent, undermining their confidence.

- **Gaslighting as care or concern:** They may manipulate you under the guise of caring for your well-being, expressing concern about your mental health or behavior. This subtle form of gaslighting can make you doubt your own perceptions and vulnerabilities, furthering their control over you.

- **Revisionist history:** They rewrite history or reinterpret past events to fit their narrative, often minimizing or dismissing your experiences and feelings. This rewriting of reality reinforces their gaslighting tactics and weakens your sense of self.

- **Emotional manipulation:** Gaslighters exploit your emotions to manipulate your behavior. They may use guilt, fear, or sympathy to gain compliance or control, leaving you feeling emotionally drained and powerless.

- **Gaslighting as "jokes" or teasing:** They disguise their manipulative behavior as harmless jokes or playful teasing, making it difficult for you to confront them or take their actions seriously. This tactic subtly undermines your confidence and boundaries over time.

- **Undermining your abilities:** They belittle your achievements, skills, or opinions, making you doubt your own competence and worth. By undermining your self-esteem, they maintain their position of superiority and control in the relationship.

- **Projection of fault:** Gaslighters deflect blame onto you for their own mistakes or shortcomings. They twist situations to make you feel guilty or responsible, further eroding your self-confidence and sense of reality.

- **Isolation tactics:** They isolate you from friends, family, or other support networks, making you increasingly dependent on them for validation and guidance. This isolation amplifies the gaslighter's influence over you and makes it harder for you to seek help or perspective from others.

Gaslighting Dynamics in Intimate Relationships

In intimate relationships, gaslighting isn't just a manipulation tactic; it's a corrosive force that distorts reality and undermines your very sense of self. Picture this: Your partner repeatedly denies facts, dismisses your emotions, and skews situations to fit their narrative. Suddenly, your own perceptions and judgments feel unreliable. You might even begin to believe that you're the one who's unstable. But let me be clear: This isn't about you. It's about them needing to gain control.

Perpetrators engaged in gaslighting within a relationship typically exhibit motivations that can be categorized in two categories: either evading accountability or attempting to manipulate the behaviors of survivors. It's not unusual to find both motivations coexisting, and occasionally intersecting.

Your partner manipulates the situation, making it seem like you're the problem, not their abusive behavior. They might shower you with affection one moment, then isolate you from friends and family the next. Their actions become unpredictable, leaving you constantly on edge. And when you try to address the issue, they twist the conversation, deflecting blame onto you.

Gaslighting thrives on making you doubt yourself. Your partner might label you as "crazy" or "overly emotional," all while painting themselves as the concerned caregiver. It's a power play, designed to keep you in line and under their thumb. And it's not just about avoiding accountability; it's about controlling every aspect of your life.

Workplace Gaslighting

Fifty-eight percent of individuals have encountered gaslighting in the workplace, a type of workplace mistreatment causing the victim to doubt themselves and their grasp of reality (*Gaslighting*, 2019).

Imagine this scenario: You're in a meeting, presenting your ideas with confidence, only to be met with ridicule and scorn from your colleagues. Your boss dismisses your contributions, belittles your achievements, and undermines your expertise at every turn. You begin to question your worth, your capabilities, and your place in the company. Welcome to the world of workplace gaslighting.

Gaslighting commonly happens within a power dynamic, like that of a manager and their subordinates. The person in power, such as a boss, can use their authority to constantly affirm their correctness, making it challenging for their employees to oppose them.

Research indicates that almost 30% of supervisors or bosses exhibit behaviors categorized as "mildly or highly toxic," with gaslighting potentially appearing as a form of toxic management (Maybray, 2023).

Behaviors from gaslighting bosses often include:

- **Undermining your confidence:** Gaslighters in the workplace will go to great lengths to undermine your confidence and self-esteem. They'll criticize your work, question your abilities, and downplay your achievements, leaving you feeling inadequate and insecure.

- **Manipulative tactics:** Gaslighters are skilled manipulators. They'll use subtle tactics like withholding information, spreading rumors, and undermining your credibility to gain control and power over you.

- **Creating a toxic environment:** Gaslighters thrive in toxic environments. They'll foster a culture of fear, intimidation, and mistrust, pitting colleagues against each other and sowing seeds of discord and chaos.

Some specific examples could include:

- avoiding transparency to catch workers off-guard (e.g., inviting you to an event that has a specific dress code and not disclosing that information)

- failing to document meeting minutes and later altering them (e.g., modifying statements from meetings to shift responsibility onto others in case of the team failing to meet their goal)

- ignoring policies except when they benefit the business (e.g., failing to address an employee complaint if doing so could damage the company's reputation)

- frequently altering objectives or job descriptions without justification (e.g., to fault employees for "underperforming")

- failing to provide comprehensive information (e.g., withholding details necessary for a worker to finish a project)

Gaslighting Among Coworkers

Gaslighting, a term used to describe someone manipulating others to assert power, is unfortunately a common occurrence in many workplaces. It can involve subtly undermining a colleague's confidence, making them doubt their own thoughts and perceptions, all with the goal of gaining advantage or climbing the corporate ladder. This behavior is often seen when people resort to tactics like belittling their colleagues or taking credit for their work, creating a toxic and competitive environment.

One common way gaslighting manifests in the workplace is through the act of kicking others down to get ahead. This manipulation technique involves discrediting the achievements and capabilities of coworkers to make oneself appear superior. For example, a colleague might take credit for a project's success in front of a manager, deliberately disregarding the contributions of others who were instrumental in its completion. This not only undermines trust among team members but also creates a sense of insecurity and fear of sabotage.

The effects of gaslighting can be detrimental to interpersonal relationships within a team. When a coworker engages in such behavior, it erodes trust and creates a hostile work environment where individuals feel constantly on edge. Imagine a scenario where a team member consistently undermines their peers' efforts during meetings, casting doubt on their competence and value. Over time, this can lead to resentment and strained relationships, hindering collaboration and productivity.

Gaslighting from coworkers can resemble:

- a coworker taking credit for your work—for example, they present your idea as their own

- creating a toxic work environment by causing issues between colleagues; this can happen when the manipulator twists one coworker's conversation about another colleague

- colleagues who intimidate by threatening to damage someone's reputation

- lying about coworkers—for example, going to the boss with false harassment claims

- undermining a colleague's confidence, such as doubting their approach or dismissing their concerns even if valid

The Effects of Workplace Gaslighting

- **Emotional distress:** Constant criticism, manipulation, and gaslighting can take a toll on your mental health. You may experience feelings of anxiety, depression, and self-doubt, leading to decreased productivity and motivation.

- **Physical symptoms:** The stress of workplace gaslighting can manifest in physical symptoms such as headaches, insomnia, and digestive issues, further exacerbating your distress and discomfort.

- **Professional stagnation:** Gaslighting can derail your career trajectory, stalling your professional growth and advancement. You may become hesitant to voice your opinions, take risks, or pursue new opportunities, fearing further ridicule and rejection.

The Use of Gaslighting and Tactics

Does any of this sound familiar? You're in a relationship where your partner constantly belittles your achievements. You came home yesterday, so excited to tell them about your promotion. Their response? "Oh calm down, it's not like they made you the CEO or anything." Do you feel like your emotions and feelings are dismissed all the time? Were you disappointed on your birthday because they didn't even acknowledge it? Did you bring it up and were you met with, "Stop being so dramatic, it's just another day."

It wasn't always this way, was it? In the beginning, you were likely gushing about how attentive this person was—the flowers, the love notes, and the constant compliments. Have you tried to have this discussion with your partner? Have you asked what happened to that romantic person? Were you told to stop being so sensitive? Or worse, were you told none of that ever happened, that you are being dramatic?

Over time, you have probably started to second-guess yourself, wondering if maybe you are too sensitive or if your memory is failing you. Before you know it, you're trapped in a web of doubt and self-blame, all orchestrated by the gaslighter.

Gaslighting Tactics

Gaslighters use a variety of tactics, each designed to slowly undermine your perception of reality:

- **Reality distortion:** You witness your partner engaging in a specific behavior, yet, when confronted, they adamantly deny it ever happening. This calculated manipulation tactic leaves you questioning everything. It's not merely a harmless fib; it's a deliberate attempt at control and manipulation. Recognizing this behavior is crucial because habitual use of such tactics signals a deeper, more insidious issue at play.

- **Conflicting statements:** Imagine you're planning a special evening based on what you believe your loved one enjoys, only to be told at the last minute that your efforts are entirely off the mark. This conflicting story, meant to cause doubt and confusion, is a classic gaslighting move. It's as if they're rewriting history right before your eyes, making you question your own sanity in the process. When faced with such contradictions, it's natural to feel disoriented and frustrated.

- **Name-calling:** This becomes a potent weapon in the hands of a gaslighter, especially when they know their target is vulnerable. If someone is already struggling with low self-esteem, the impact of derogatory remarks can be devastating.

Gaslighters exploit this vulnerability, weaponizing words to further erode their victim's self-worth and sense of reality. They tend to hit where they know it will hurt. If you have issues with your weight, they will call you horrid names to body-shame you. If you're worried about being a good parent, they will be sure to call you a bad one.

- **Pitting individuals against each other:** This is another sinister tactic employed by gaslighters to maintain control. By manipulating perceptions and stirring up discord between two people, the gaslighter effectively maintains their position of power. Whether it's in a workplace setting or within personal relationships, this divide-and-conquer strategy aims to keep everyone off-balance and dependent on the gaslighter's approval. You might also hear, "You know she agrees with me about this; she even told me she also believes you are too emotional."

- **Intentional changes in behavior:** This serves as a red flag for gaslighting. When someone behaves drastically differently depending on the audience, it's a clear sign of manipulation. If they shower you with affection in public but turn cruel and dismissive in private, it's not just inconsistency—it's a deliberate attempt to keep you off-balance and under their thumb. For instance, if your partner compliments you and pays you positive attention during a family barbeque, yet the car ride home is filled with name-calling and deflection, you are being gaslit.

- **Deflection:** Deflection is a favored tactic of gaslighters to evade accountability and control the narrative. By redirecting conversations or turning the focus back on their target, they aim to cause confusion and frustration. Questions are met with accusations, leaving the victim feeling unheard and invalidated. It's a relentless cycle designed to keep the gaslighter in control at all costs. Let's say you find some concerning text messages on your partner's phone. When you ask about them, you're met with anger and accusations. "Why are you going through my phone? Don't you trust me? If we don't have trust, we might as well end everything right now!"

- **Scapegoating:** Scapegoating is the ultimate blame game, where the gaslighter shifts responsibility onto their victim for their own shortcomings. Even when it's clear the gaslighter is at fault, they'll find a way to twist the narrative and make their target feel culpable. It's a cunning strategy aimed at undermining confidence and fostering dependence on the gaslighter's version of reality.

Is Gaslighting Ever Ethical?

Can gaslighting ever be justified ethically? Let's delve into this territory with clarity and precision.

First, let's be unequivocal: Gaslighting is fundamentally unethical. It preys on vulnerability, exploits trust, and undermines the very foundation of healthy relationships. Whether it's in personal relationships, workplaces, or broader societal dynamics, gaslighting corrodes the fabric of trust and mutual respect.

Now, let's entertain the notion of whether there could be a scenario where gaslighting might seem ethical—perhaps in the context of protecting someone from harm or delivering a harsh truth for their own good? While these scenarios may seem plausible on the surface, they quickly unravel upon closer examination.

Consider this—gaslighting under the guise of protection is still manipulation. It's wielding power over someone else's perception and reality without their consent. True protection and genuine concern can be achieved through open communication, empathy, and respect for autonomy, not through psychological manipulation.

Moreover, the consequences of gaslighting can be severe and long-lasting. The collateral damage inflicted by gaslighting far outweighs any perceived short-term benefits.

So, where does this leave us? We must strive to foster ethical relationships built on trust, honesty, and mutual respect. Challenge the toxic norms that perpetuate manipulation and gaslighting. Lead by example, championing authenticity and integrity in your interactions.

Strategies for Protecting Yourself From Gaslighting

You can arm yourself with strategies that not only protect you but also empower you to stand firm in your truth. Let's delve into assertiveness and boundary setting as powerful shields against gaslighting.

Assertiveness

Assertiveness is a vital tool in the battle against gaslighting, empowering you to reclaim control over your reality and safeguard your mental well-being.

When you assert yourself, you send a clear message to the gaslighter that you refuse to be manipulated. By confidently expressing your thoughts, feelings, and needs, you establish a firm foundation of self-assurance. This self-assurance acts as a barrier against their attempts to distort your reality. When you assertively communicate your truth, you reinforce your sense of identity and strengthen your resilience against their gaslighting tactics.

Noah has been in a relationship with Jane for two years. About six months into dating, he notices Jane's behavior changing, including frequent belittling remarks, invalidation of his feelings, and manipulation of facts to make him doubt his own memory.

Noah demonstrates courage and resilience as he learns to assert himself against the gaslighting tactics of his partner. He starts to take proactive steps toward reclaiming his sense of self and healing.

Examples of Assertiveness

- **Recognition of gaslighting behavior:** Noah begins to recognize the patterns of gaslighting in his relationship with Jane. He notices how she often dismisses his concerns, blames him for misunderstandings, and denies previous conversations or promises.

- **Internal reflection:** Noah takes some time to reflect on his experiences and acknowledges the impact of gaslighting on his mental and emotional well-being. He realizes that he deserves to be treated with respect and that Jane's behavior is not acceptable.

- **Seeking support:** Noah confides in his close friend Cameron about his concerns regarding Jane's behavior. Cameron listens attentively and validates Noah's feelings, reassuring him that he's not alone and that he deserves better treatment in his relationship.

- **Setting boundaries:** Empowered by his friend's support, Noah decides to set boundaries with Jane. During a calm and assertive conversation, he communicates his feelings directly to her and expresses his boundaries regarding respectful communication and honesty in their relationship.

- **Standing firm:** When Jane attempts to gaslight him during their conversation, Noah remains firm in his convictions and refuses to be swayed by her manipulative tactics. He calmly repeats his boundaries and insists on being treated with respect.

- **Seeking professional help:** Recognizing the complexity of his situation, Noah decides to seek professional help from a therapist who specializes in relational dynamics and emotional abuse. In therapy, he explores the underlying issues in his relationship with Jane and learns coping strategies to assert himself and protect his mental well-being.

- **Continued growth:** Through therapy and ongoing self-reflection, Noah continues to grow in his assertiveness and self-confidence. He learns to trust his instincts, set healthy boundaries, and prioritize his own well-being.

Setting Boundaries

Boundary setting serves as a protective shield against gaslighting. By defining and asserting your boundaries, you establish clear parameters for acceptable behavior. Gaslighters often thrive on blurring boundaries and overstepping limits, but when you assert your boundaries, you establish firm lines that cannot be crossed. This sends a powerful message that your self-respect and well-being are non-negotiable.

Moreover, maintaining firm boundaries demonstrates self-respect and self-worth, signaling to the gaslighter that you value yourself enough to protect your mental and emotional health. This can deter further attempts at manipulation, as gaslighters often target those they perceive as vulnerable or lacking in self-confidence.

In essence, assertiveness and boundary setting are proactive measures that help you to assert your reality, protect your boundaries, and safeguard your mental well-being against the insidious tactics of gaslighting. When you embody assertiveness and boundary setting, you assert your power, reclaim your identity, and refuse to be swayed by the gaslighter's attempts to distort your truth.

Seeking Support and Professional Help

For some, professional help is what's needed to start healing. We can find ourselves in situations with gaslighters who are toxic, manipulative, and, at times, dangerous. Seeking support or professional help is a crucial step for anyone who has been the victim of this kind of gaslighting. Here's an outline of how you can take action:

- **Recognize the signs:** Before seeking help, it's essential to recognize that you've been a victim of gaslighting. Reflect on your experiences and acknowledge any patterns of manipulation, doubt, or confusion in your interactions with others.

- **Reach out:** Start by confiding in trusted friends, family members, or peers who can provide emotional support and validation. Sharing your experiences with someone you trust can help validate your reality and provide a sense of reassurance.

- **Consider help:** If the effects of gaslighting are impacting your mental health and well-being, consider seeking professional help from a therapist, counselor, or mental health professional. These professionals are trained to help individuals navigate the complex dynamics of gaslighting and provide support tailored to your specific needs.

- **Research therapists or counselors:** Take the time to research therapists or counselors who specialize in trauma, abuse, or relational dynamics. Look for professionals who have experience working with individuals who have experienced gaslighting and who offer evidence-based therapeutic approaches.

- **Schedule an initial consultation:** Reach out to potential therapists or counselors to schedule an initial consultation. During this meeting, you can discuss your concerns and your goals for therapy and determine if the therapist is the right fit for you.

- **Participate in therapy:** If you decide to proceed with therapy, actively participate in the therapeutic process. Be open and honest with your therapist about your experiences, thoughts, and feelings. Therapy can provide a safe space to explore your experiences, develop coping strategies, and rebuild self-esteem.

- **Explore support groups:** Consider joining support groups or online communities for those who have experienced gaslighting or emotional abuse. Connecting with others who have similar experiences can provide validation, solidarity, and a sense of belonging.

- **Practice self-care:** Engage in self-care activities that nurture your mental, emotional, and physical well-being. This may include activities such as exercise, mindfulness, journaling, or spending time with supportive friends and loved ones.

- **Monitor your progress:** Keep track of your progress and any changes in your thoughts, feelings, and behaviors over time. Celebrate your achievements and milestones, no matter how small, as you continue to heal and grow from the effects of gaslighting.

Remember, asking for help does not make you vulnerable or weak but rather courageous, because you are reclaiming your sense of self and rebuilding your life after gaslighting. You deserve to live a life free from manipulation and doubt, and support is available to help you heal.

Interactive Element: The Big Picture

This discussion isn't mere theoretical musing; it's a strategic endeavor to fortify your mental fortress. As we revisit the A.M.E.L.I.O.R.A.T.E. framework, remind yourself that each letter represents a step toward self-improvement and protection. Here, we've visited the sixth phase: "Overtures of gaslighting."

Gaslighting, with its treacherous dance of distortion and deception, is a dangerous weapon in the arsenal of psychological manipulation. But, armed with knowledge, you can dismantle its power over you.

Let's zoom out for a moment and connect the dots. In understanding gaslighting, we're not just dissecting the tactics of manipulation; we're honing our awareness of human psychology. By recognizing the signs and patterns of gaslighting, you're not not only defending against manipulation but also gaining insight into the intricacies of human behavior.

As we conclude this chapter, remember that knowledge is your greatest weapon against manipulation. When you continue to educate yourself about dark psychology, you're not succumbing to fear; you're embracing empowerment. So, let's continue this journey of self-discovery and protection, armed with the insights gleaned from the study of gaslighting.

Next up, we're building an entire tool kit to fight psychological warfare. Turn the page and get ready to arm yourself for the life you deserve.

Chapter 7:

Reframing Your Tool Kit for

Psychological Warfare

Dark psychology is the art of making others dance to the tune of your desires, while they believe they are leading the way. —Friedrich Engels

We are now entering the seventh phase of the A.M.E.L.I.O.R.A.T.E. framework, where we uncover the art of psychological warfare and equip you with the tools necessary to handle social interaction.

It's not enough to merely recognize the techniques of psychological warfare; you must also be prepared to counter them with skill and finesse. This requires a multifaceted approach drawing from various disciplines.

So, ask yourself if you're ready to arm yourself with knowledge and strength, to stand firm in the face of psychological adversity? If so, then let us begin. Victory and empowerment are within reach.

Principles of Psychological Warfare

Psychological warfare evokes images of espionage, military strategies, and covert operations. Although it is vital in those fields, it also influences the lives of ordinary people in often unnoticed ways.

Psychological warfare, commonly shortened to "psywar," utilizes a variety of strategies to control and shape the beliefs, ideas, and feelings of people and communities. It serves multiple objectives, including military and political aims as well as commercial and promotional endeavors.

Psychological warfare impacts ordinary people across various levels, usually in a subtle and sneaky manner. Let's uncover several areas where its influence can be significant:

- **Advertising:** Advertising agencies commonly use psychological tactics to persuade individuals to purchase products they might not actually require. This involves generating artificial desires, endorsing "FOMO" (fear of missing out), and employing emotional cues to impact buying choices.

- **Politics:** Political campaigns utilize psychological tactics to influence public perception, garner backing, or tarnish adversaries. Common strategies include disseminating misinformation, instigating fear, and leveraging emotional appeals.

- **Social media:** Social media platforms utilize algorithms to maintain user engagement, potentially fostering addictive behaviors and exposure to partial or deceptive content, which can ultimately influence individuals' perspectives and social connections.

- **News media:** The news media frequently focuses on sensational stories to attract attention, which can result in heightened anxiety and fear within the general public. Techniques such as misleading headlines, clickbait, and emotional manipulation are employed to increase viewership.

- **Cyberbullying and online harassment:** Individuals can face psychological warfare on a personal level in the form of cyberbullying and online harassment, leading to significant emotional and mental health impacts.

- **Peer pressure and conformity:** In social environments, peer pressure and societal norms may manipulate behavior, causing individuals to adhere to unhealthy or unethical standards.

When Is Psychological Warfare Needed?

Psychological warfare isn't about coercion or deception—it's about understanding human behavior and leveraging that knowledge to achieve strategic objectives. It's about wielding empathy, insight, and influence with precision and integrity. Let's look at some everyday examples.

Corporate Settings

Let's examine the intricacies of business dynamics and the strategic implementation of psychological insights to gain an edge:

- **Negotiations:** Imagine sitting across the table, staring into the eyes of your adversary. Understanding their psyche can be the key to unlocking favorable terms. By discerning their strengths, weaknesses, and motivations, you can craft a negotiation strategy that tilts the scales in your favor. Are they driven by ego or logic? Do they prioritize short-term gains or long-term relationships? By answering these questions, you can navigate the negotiation battlefield with precision and finesse.

- **Leadership transitions:** In the ever-evolving landscape of corporate hierarchies, leadership changes are inevitable. Whether you're ascending to the throne or orchestrating a seamless transition, psychological warfare can be your ally. Managing perceptions, expectations, and emotions can mean the difference between a smooth handover of power and a turbulent upheaval. How do you ensure continuity while instilling confidence in your leadership? By leveraging psychological strategies to cultivate trust, rally support, and inspire loyalty.

- **Conflict resolution:** Within the crucible of corporate culture, conflicts are bound to arise. From clashes of egos to power struggles, navigating these turbulent waters requires skill and tact. Here, psychological warfare isn't about manipulation; it's about strategic communication and emotional intelligence. How do you defuse tensions before they escalate into full-blown crises? When you understand the underlying motivations, grievances, and dynamics at play, you can orchestrate resolutions that preserve harmony and foster collaboration.

Social Situations

In the following examples, the key lies not in manipulation for personal gain but in leveraging psychological insights for constructive purposes. It's about fostering empathy, building trust, and enhancing communication skills to navigate the complexities of human interaction effectively:

- **Navigating personal relationships:** In the intricate dance of personal relationships, understanding the undercurrents of emotions and motivations is crucial. Psychological warfare in this context doesn't entail manipulation for selfish gain but rather strategic empathy and communication. When conflicts arise, knowing how to de-escalate tensions, empathize with others' perspectives, and assert boundaries can be similar to wielding psychological armor. By mastering these skills, you can foster healthier, more resilient relationships. Take a moment to reflect on how you can harness psychological insights to strengthen bonds and foster genuine connections in your personal relationships.

- **Social influence and persuasion:** Whether you're vying for a promotion, negotiating with colleagues, or simply aiming to be heard and respected in group settings, the art of social influence is invaluable. This arena of psychological warfare involves understanding the intricacies of persuasion, charisma, and social dynamics. It's about knowing when to assert yourself with conviction, when to listen actively, and when to adapt your communication style to sway opinions and garner support. Ask yourself how can you leverage psychological principles to enhance your persuasive abilities and influence others positively.

Marketing and Public Relations

When does the battlefield of psychological warfare extend its reach into the spaces of marketing and public relations? It's not just about military maneuvers or political intrigue; it's about shaping perceptions, influencing decisions, and, ultimately, securing dominance in the minds of the masses. In the cutthroat world of business, psychological tactics become indispensable tools in the arsenal of marketers and public relations professionals alike. Let's explore the trenches and understand when and why psychological warfare becomes a necessity in these domains:

- **Brand perception:** Imagine that you're launching a new product into a market saturated with competitors vying for attention. How do you stand out? It's not merely about having a superior product; it's about crafting a narrative that captivates, resonates, and, ultimately, convinces consumers to choose you over the rest. This is where psychological warfare comes into play. By leveraging principles from psychology, marketers can tap into the subconscious desires and emotions of their target audience. From the colors used in branding to the language employed in advertisements, every element is meticulously designed to elicit specific responses. It's about creating an emotional connection that transcends mere product features, embedding a brand into the psyche of consumers. Psychological warfare in branding extends beyond mere allure; it's about shaping perceptions over time. Through consistent messaging and strategic storytelling, marketers mold how the public perceives their brand. Whether it's projecting an image of luxury, reliability, or innovation, every interaction with the brand is carefully choreographed to reinforce these desired associations.

- **Crisis management:** In the tumultuous landscape of modern business, crises are an inevitability. Whether it's a product recall, a PR scandal, or a financial downturn, how an organization handles these challenges can make or break its reputation. This is where psychological warfare takes on a defensive stance, aiming to protect and preserve the integrity of the brand. When crisis strikes, the battleground shifts from product promotion to damage control. It's a high-stakes game of perception management, where every move is scrutinized by the public and competitors alike. Here, the principles of psychology come into play in a different capacity. It's about understanding the psychology of crisis response—how emotions influence public opinion, how narratives are shaped, and how trust is either reinforced or eroded. Effective crisis management requires a delicate balance of transparency, empathy, and strategic communication. It's about projecting an image of accountability while simultaneously reassuring stakeholders of your ability to weather the storm. Through carefully crafted messages and calculated media appearances, organizations can steer the narrative in their favor, mitigating reputational damage and safeguarding long-term trust.

Competitive Sports

Imagine yourself on the field, your heart racing, adrenaline pumping, and every move scrutinized by opponents hungry for victory. In this high-stakes environment, mastering the art of psychological manipulation can mean the difference between triumph and defeat:

- **Intimidation tactics:** Intimidation is a cornerstone of psychological warfare in sports. Picture yourself facing off against a rival team or opponent exuding an aura of unshakeable confidence. Their mere presence instills doubt and hesitation in your mind, subtly tipping the scales of the game in their favor. But what if you could turn the tables? When you utilize the principles of dark psychology, you can project an aura of invincibility, instilling fear and uncertainty in your adversaries.

- **Performance psychology:** This offers another avenue for gaining a competitive edge. Imagine being able to harness the power of your mind to enhance your physical abilities and mental resilience. Through techniques such as visualization, positive self-talk, and goal setting, you can foster a mindset primed for success, capable of overcoming even the most daunting challenges. But beware—just as you can use these techniques to bolster your own performance, so too can your opponents. Recognize and neutralize their psychological tactics, allowing you to maintain your focus and composure in the face of adversity.

Political Arenas

In the political arena, psychological warfare becomes a tool of necessity, a means to shape narratives, influence minds, and, ultimately, secure power. Let's explore why:

- **Elections and campaigns:** Picture a political battleground where perceptions are weapons and narratives are artillery. Here, psychological warfare reigns supreme. Candidates meticulously craft their personas, messages, and promises to sway the hearts and minds of voters. Every speech, every ad, every debate is a strategic move in a psychological chess game aimed at capturing the public's trust and, ultimately, their votes. But beware, for behind the scenes lurks manipulation in its subtlest forms. From targeted advertisements tailored to exploit psychological vulnerabilities to orchestrated smear campaigns designed to tarnish opponents' reputations, the political landscape is rife with psychological tactics aimed at gaining an edge.

- **Legislative debates:** Within the hallowed halls of legislative bodies, where laws are forged and destinies shaped, psychological warfare takes on a different guise. Here, it's about swaying opinions, rallying allies, and thwarting adversaries. Lobbyists and interest groups employ an arsenal of persuasion techniques, from framing issues in a favorable light to exploiting cognitive biases, all in the pursuit of influencing policy decisions. Public opinion becomes a battleground, and those who master the art of psychological manipulation hold the keys to legislative success.

- **International diplomacy:** Beyond domestic borders lies a theater of geopolitical maneuvering where nations vie for supremacy and influence. In the world of international diplomacy, psychological warfare becomes a tool of statecraft, wielded by diplomats and leaders alike to project strength, negotiate from positions of advantage, and shape the global narrative. From carefully curated public appearances designed to convey authority to strategic leaks and misinformation campaigns aimed at sowing discord among adversaries, psychological tactics play a pivotal role in shaping the outcomes of diplomatic engagements.

Strategic Thinking and Planning: Psychological Warfare Techniques

In the intricate game of psychological warfare, understanding the principles is not merely advantageous—it's essential. But what are these principles, and how can they be wielded effectively to not only protect yourself but also to navigate the complex social landscapes with strategy?

Anticipatory Thinking

The cornerstone of psychological warfare, this is about being proactive rather than reactive, anticipating the moves of your adversaries before they even make them by honing your ability to foresee potential scenarios and pre-emptive responses.

Anticipatory thinking isn't just a cognitive skill; it's a psychological warfare technique, and a valuable one. Think about it: In the military, intelligence agencies, business, medicine, and social services, those who excel in anticipatory thinking hold a significant advantage. They're the ones who can anticipate moves before they happen, predict outcomes, and strategize accordingly.

It's about more than just reacting to what's happening around you. It's about proactively analyzing the motives, patterns, and vulnerabilities of those who seek to manipulate you. It's about being aware of the various futures that could unfold, from the plausible to the preposterous, and preparing accordingly.

Just as organizations and governments project societal and ecological needs into a preferred future, so too must you project your mental defenses into a preferred state. Anticipatory thinking empowers you to foster preparedness for adverse events, to fortify your psychological resilience, and to drive innovation in your own mental defenses.

So, how do you master anticipatory thinking? It starts with developing a deep understanding of the dark arts of manipulation. Educate yourself on the tactics commonly employed by manipulators: gaslighting, guilt-tripping, love bombing, and more. Arm yourself with knowledge, for it is the ultimate weapon against deception.

Next, hone your intuition. Pay attention to those subtle red flags, those whispers of doubt that tug at the corners of your mind. Trust your gut instinct, for it is often your first line of defense against manipulation. But perhaps most importantly, practice self-awareness. Understand your own vulnerabilities, your triggers, your blind spots.

Anticipatory thinking is not just a skill; it's a mindset. It's about taking control of your own mental landscape, refusing to be swayed by the whims of others. So, arm yourself with knowledge, trust your instincts, and stay vigilant.

Psychological Profiling

This is the art of understanding human behavior to predict, influence, and control it. Start by mastering self-awareness. Know your strengths, weaknesses, triggers, and vulnerabilities. Understand how you react under stress, pressure, or manipulation. By knowing yourself, you can pre-emptively recognize when someone is trying to manipulate you.

Next, hone your observation skills. Pay attention to people's words, actions, and body language. Notice inconsistencies, patterns, and deviations from the norm. This keen awareness allows you to spot potential manipulators before they ensnare you in their web of deceit.

Scenario Planning

You're thrust into a social or professional situation where subtle cues indicate manipulation at play. Your gut churns, sensing danger, but uncertainty clouds your judgment. What do you do? React impulsively, or take charge with strategic foresight?

Here's where scenario planning becomes your shield against psychological onslaughts. Instead of being a mere pawn in someone else's game, you become the master strategist of your own destiny:

- **Step one: Heightened awareness.** By immersing yourself in the principles of dark psychology, you illuminate the shadows where manipulation lurks. Understand the subtle signs—the gaslighter's tactics, the psychological triggers, the power dynamics at play. Ask yourself: What are the warning signs? How can you spot manipulation before it traps you?

- **Step two: Strategic anticipation.** Envision potential scenarios, from subtle gaslighting to overt manipulation. Map out the players, their motives, and the potential outcomes. Anticipate their moves like a grandmaster plotting their next chess move. How might they try to bend reality to their will? How can you counter their tactics?

- **Step three: Tactical preparation.** Arm yourself with a repertoire of responses tailored to each scenario. From assertive communication to boundary setting, equip yourself with psychological defenses. Practice self-affirmation and confidence-building techniques to fortify your mental resilience. What strategies can you deploy to maintain your autonomy and protect your psyche?

- **Step four: Dynamic adaptation.** In the heat of the moment, remain flexible yet resolute. Stay attuned to shifts in the psychological landscape and adjust your tactics accordingly. Trust your instincts, but also rely on the strategic framework you've meticulously crafted. How can you navigate the complexities of human interaction with agility and poise?

By embracing scenario planning, you transcend the role of mere observer, becoming an active participant in shaping your reality. You pre-empt manipulation, seizing control of the narrative with strategic grace and tactical foresight.

When you master these principles, you can transcend mere reaction and become a masterful architect of your own destiny. With a proactive approach, you can navigate complex social landscapes with grace and foresight, ensuring success in both personal and professional arenas.

How to Always Be Three Steps Ahead

Within the world of psychological warfare, being three steps ahead is not just advantageous; it's crucial for self-preservation. Here's a blueprint to always stay ahead, safeguarding your mental and emotional well-being from the pernicious effects of manipulation:

- **Forecasting potential moves:** Begin by cultivating a keen awareness of human behavior. Anticipate potential actions by understanding underlying motives. Ask yourself: What are their goals? What drives their behavior? By analyzing situational cues and psychological triggers, you can forecast their next move with remarkable accuracy. Remember, in the arena of manipulation, actions are often orchestrated with precision to achieve specific outcomes. Your ability to anticipate these moves grants you a strategic advantage.

- **Leveraging psychological profiling:** Dive deep into the psyche of those around you. Understand their personality traits, strengths, weaknesses, and vulnerabilities. Consider their past experiences, traumas, and triggers. This psychological profiling enables you to tailor your responses and influence their perceptions subtly. By crafting your approach based on their psychological makeup, you subtly guide the interaction's trajectory, steering it in your favor. Remember, knowledge is your friend, and in the world of manipulation, understanding the human psyche is the same as having a weapon at your disposal.

- **Analyzing historical behavior patterns:** History often repeats itself, especially when discussing human behavior. Take note of recurring patterns in their actions and reactions. Have they employed similar tactics in the past? How did you respond, and what were the outcomes? By dissecting past interactions, you gain invaluable insights into their *modus operandi*. This retrospective analysis equips you with a strategic road map, enabling you to pre-empt their moves effectively. Remember, patterns provide clues to future behavior. By deciphering these patterns, you position yourself strategically, pre-empting their maneuvers and maintaining control of the narrative.

- **Continuous learning and adaptation:** Picture this: You're standing on shifting sands, constantly evolving and adapting to the ever-changing landscape. In the realm of psychological warfare, stagnation is synonymous with vulnerability. Embrace the ethos of continuous learning. Educate yourself about the tactics of manipulation, dissecting the psychology behind them. Stay updated on the latest research and insights into human behavior. But don't stop there: Apply this knowledge in real-world scenarios, honing your ability to recognize and resist manipulation techniques as they manifest.

- **Feedback loops:** Imagine a finely tuned instrument, sensitive to the slightest nuances of its environment. Similarly, cultivate a feedback loop within yourself. Develop a heightened awareness of your emotional responses and behavioral patterns. Pay attention to subtle cues that may indicate manipulation attempts. Utilize introspection and self-reflection to assess the impact of external influences on your thoughts and actions. By establishing this internal feedback mechanism, you empower yourself to detect and deflect manipulation in its infancy.

- **Skill development:** Think of yourself as a psychological martial artist, mastering the art of self-defense against manipulation. Nurture a diverse skill set that encompasses emotional intelligence, critical thinking, and assertiveness. Sharpen your ability to analyze information critically, discerning fact from fiction within the noise of manipulation tactics. Practice effective communication techniques, assertively asserting your boundaries and convictions. Invest in your personal development, building resilience and confidence.

- **Environmental scanning:** Always keep a keen eye on changes in your surroundings that could impact your strategies and well-being. Stay attuned to shifts in social dynamics, organizational hierarchies, and broader socioeconomic trends. Recognize that the tactics of manipulation are often context-dependent, adapting to exploit vulnerabilities within specific environments. When you maintain a proactive stance and anticipate potential threats, you position yourself to effectively counteract manipulation attempts before they gain traction.

- **Choice architecture:** Picture this: You walk into a store and, before you know it, you're drawn to a particular product. Was it your choice, or were you subtly nudged toward it? That's the essence of choice architecture, the strategic arrangement of options to influence decisions. To protect yourself from manipulation through choice architecture, awareness is key. Train yourself to recognize when choices are being presented in a way that guides you toward a specific outcome. Pause, evaluate your options independently, and consider whether your decision aligns with your genuine preferences and values.

- **Expectation management:** How often have you found yourself disappointed because reality didn't meet your expectations? Expectation management is about shaping perceptions to align with desired outcomes. In psychological warfare, this can involve setting unrealistic expectations with the aim of manipulating behavior or controlling reactions. To safeguard against this tactic, cultivate a healthy skepticism. Question overly optimistic promises or exaggerated claims. Take a step back and critically assess whether the expectations being set are reasonable and grounded in reality. By doing so, you fortify your mental defenses against manipulation.

- **Information control:** In the age of information overload, the power to control what information reaches us is a potent weapon. Those adept at psychological warfare know this all too well. When you carefully manage the flow of information, you can shape narratives, influence opinions, and manipulate decisions. To shield yourself from manipulation through information control, become a discerning consumer of information. Question the sources, motives, and potential biases behind the information presented to you. Seek out diverse perspectives and actively engage in critical thinking. Stay informed and be vigilant. This can help you be resistant to attempts to sway your beliefs or actions.

The Responsible Use of Psychological Tactics

So, how do you wield the tactics of dark psychology while remaining morally responsible?

First, recognize the power dynamics at play. Are you in a position of authority or influence over others? If so, understand the immense responsibility that comes with it. Manipulating those who trust you or depend on you is a breach of that trust and can lead to significant harm. Ask yourself: Are you using your influence for the betterment of others, or are you exploiting it for personal gain?

Next, consider the intent behind your actions. Are you seeking to manipulate for selfish reasons, such as gaining power or control? Or are you using these techniques to protect yourself or others from harm? Intent matters greatly in ethical decision-making. If your motives are driven by compassion and protection, you're more likely to use these techniques with integrity.

Furthermore, transparency is key. Are you being honest about your intentions and the methods you're employing? Deception and deceit erode trust and can have long-lasting consequences. If you're engaging in psychological tactics, ensure that all parties involved are aware of what's happening and why. This allows for informed consent and prevents feelings of betrayal.

Another crucial consideration is the impact of your actions. Are you causing undue harm or distress to others? While manipulation can sometimes be necessary for self-defense or protection, it's essential to minimize harm wherever possible. Consider the potential consequences of your tactics and strive to mitigate any negative effects on those involved.

Last, self-reflection is paramount. Constantly evaluate your motives, your methods, and the effects of your actions. Are you staying true to your values and principles? Are you willing to reassess and course-correct if you realize you've strayed from ethical conduct? Hold yourself accountable and be willing to confront any ethical dilemmas that arise.

Using psychological warfare techniques with ethics and morals requires a mindful approach. Consider power dynamics, intent, transparency, impact, and self-reflection as guiding principles. By prioritizing integrity and compassion, you can navigate the complexities of manipulation while safeguarding the well-being of yourself and others.

Interactive Element: The Big Picture

Picture this: You're standing at the helm of your own psychological fortress, fortified by the A.M.E.L.I.O.R.A.T.E. framework. You've arrived at the pinnacle of the seventh phase: "Reframing your tool kit for psychological warfare."

Reframing isn't just about shuffling around your mental furniture; it's about revolutionizing your approach to self-protection. It's about understanding that every tactic, every strategy, every insight gleaned from exploring dark psychology serves a singular purpose: to fortify your defenses and empower you against the machinations of psychological predators.

Think of it as upgrading your arsenal. Each concept explored, from manipulation techniques to the subtle art of gaslighting, adds another layer to your protective shield. But it's not just about defense; it's about offense too. By understanding the tactics used against you, you gain the upper hand, turning the tables on would-be manipulators.

So, remember this: Each tactic, each strategy, is a piece of the puzzle, a tool in your kit. But it's up to you to wield them wisely to safeguard your mind and protect your psyche. With the A.M.E.L.I.O.R.A.T.E. framework as your guide, you're not just a passive observer; you're an active participant in the battle for your own psychological sovereignty.

In the next chapter, we'll uncover the art of resilience—how to bounce back stronger than ever after enduring manipulation or harm. Discover the transformative power of resilience as we explore actionable strategies to rebuild your mental fortitude and emerge from adversity with newfound strength.

So, set yourself for the challenges ahead, for with each trial overcome, you're one step closer to mastery over the intricate dance of psychological warfare.

Chapter 8:

Accessing Resilience Post-

Manipulation

In the realm of dark psychology, trust is a commodity to be bought and sold. –
George Orwell

We now start the eighth phase of the A.M.E.L.I.O.R.A.T.E. framework. Here, we uncover the heart of psychological resilience after experiencing the treacherous terrain of manipulation and gaslighting. We now know this can leave even the most steadfast people reeling in its aftermath. But resilience is not just a trait; it's a skill that can be honed, nurtured, and strengthened.

Resilience doesn't involve disregarding the pain or acting as if the manipulation was a figment of your imagination. It requires recognizing the truth of your situation and not allowing it to determine who you are. It means acknowledging your inner strength and ability to move through the challenges, even when faced with adversity. How can you tap into this wellspring of resilience inside you?

Are you ready to find out?

Utilizing Dark Psychology for Self-Protection

In the intricate dance of manipulation, one of the most pervasive tactics is the attempt to dominate or alter your frame of reference. Your frame, the lens through which you interpret the world, is a powerful tool that shapes your perceptions and judgments. It's the cornerstone of your identity, guiding your decisions and reactions.

Let's say you firmly believe in maintaining a healthy work–life balance, valuing yourself as a diligent employee who respects boundaries. Yet, your boss insists that true dedication entails sacrificing personal time for work. Suddenly, your frame is under siege. Are you still a valued employee if your principles clash with the company's demands? Such subtle assaults on your frame are the hallmark of manipulation.

You need to maintain your frame at all costs. Your beliefs, your values—they are sacrosanct. Don't yield to pressure or coercion. If uncertainty clouds your judgment, take a step back. Request time to reflect, to reaffirm your stance. Remember, your frame, your ideals, and your opinions are non-negotiable.

Knowledge will always be your strongest armor. Understanding dark psychology isn't just about recognizing when you're being manipulated; it's about reclaiming your power and defending yourself against those who seek to exploit it:

- **Awareness is key:** The first step in defending yourself against dark psychology tactics is recognizing them when they occur. Educate yourself on the techniques commonly used by manipulators: gaslighting, cognitive dissonance, projection, and many more. Understand the subtle cues and behaviors that signal manipulation in action. Awareness is your early warning system, allowing you to nip manipulation in the bud before it takes root.

- **Trust your instincts:** Your intuition is a powerful tool in the fight against manipulation. If something feels off in a relationship or interaction, don't ignore it. Trust your gut and investigate further. Manipulators often rely on creating doubt and confusion, but your instincts can cut through the fog of manipulation and guide you to the truth.

- **Establish boundaries:** Manipulators thrive on blurring boundaries and invading personal space. Take a stand by establishing clear boundaries and enforcing them consistently. This could mean saying no to unreasonable requests, limiting contact with toxic individuals, or setting guidelines for acceptable behavior in your relationships. Boundaries act as a barrier, protecting your mental and emotional well-being from manipulation.

- **Practice self-care:** Manipulation can take a toll on your mental health and self-esteem. Make self-care a priority in your life. Engage in activities that bring you joy and relaxation, surround yourself with supportive friends and family, and seek professional help if needed. A strong sense of self-worth is your best defense against manipulation tactics aimed at undermining your confidence and autonomy.

- **Develop critical thinking skills:** Manipulators often rely on logical fallacies and emotional manipulation to control their targets. Sharpen your critical thinking skills to see through their tactics. Question information presented to you, analyze arguments critically, and don't be swayed by appeals to emotion or authority. By thinking critically, you can resist manipulation and make informed decisions based on reason and evidence.

- **Seek support:** You don't have to face manipulation alone. Reach out to trusted friends, family members, or mental health professionals for support and guidance. Talking about your experiences can help validate your feelings and provide perspective on the situation. Surround yourself with a strong support network that uplifts and empowers you to stand firm against manipulation.

Incorporating these strategies into your life equips you with the tools you need to defend yourself against manipulation and gaslighting. In the end, it's about empowerment. By dismantling manipulation, you reclaim autonomy. You become impervious to coercion, a force to be reckoned with. And in the crucible of confrontation, you emerge not only unscathed but strengthened. For when you master the art of defense, you not only earn the respect of others but, more importantly, you earn your own self-respect.

The Thin Line Between Self-Defense and Manipulation

Within human interaction, the line between self-defense and manipulation can often seem perilously thin. Understanding this distinction is vital for safeguarding your mental and emotional well-being.

Self-defense in the psychological world involves protecting yourself from harm, whether it be emotional manipulation, gaslighting, or other forms of coercion. It's about setting boundaries, asserting your needs, and maintaining your freedom. True self-defense operates from a place of authenticity and integrity. It's about safeguarding yourself without infringing upon the rights or well-being of others.

On the flip side, manipulation is a dark art, a sinister game where someone seeks to control, deceive, and exploit others for personal gain. As we've discussed, it's a subtle erosion of that freedom, a toxic dance of power and deceit. Manipulation operates under the guise of self-defense but is rooted in deception and selfish motives.

So, how do you distinguish between the two?

First, examine the intent behind your actions. Are you seeking to protect yourself and assert your boundaries, or are you manipulating others to serve your own agenda? Intent is the compass that guides your actions; ensure it points toward integrity and genuine self-preservation.

Next, scrutinize the means you employ. Self-defense relies on open communication, assertiveness, and healthy boundaries. It's about standing firm in your convictions without resorting to deceit or coercion. Conversely, manipulation thrives on deception, guilt-tripping, and exploitation. It's a game of psychological chess where honesty takes a backseat to control.

Furthermore, consider the impact of your actions. Are you fostering mutual respect and understanding, or are you causing distrust and discord? Self-defense builds bridges; manipulation burns them. It's essential to be mindful of the ripple effects your behavior may have on others' well-being.

In essence, the thin line between self-defense and manipulation boils down to authenticity versus deceit, empowerment versus exploitation. To walk the path of genuine self-protection, cultivate self-awareness, empathy, and ethical discernment. Arm yourself with knowledge of psychological tactics, but wield them with integrity and empathy. And remember, true strength lies not in manipulation but in the courage to stand tall in your truth, come what may.

The Consequences of Unethical Practices

It's time to confront the harsh realities of unethical manipulation. When wielded without conscience or restraint, dark psychological tactics can wreak havoc on people and society as a whole.

First, understand that the consequences of unethical practices in dark psychology are profound and far-reaching. They corrode the very fabric of trust and undermine the fundamental pillars of healthy human interaction.

Imagine a world where every interaction is laced with hidden agendas and ulterior motives. In such a landscape, genuine connections become scarce commodities, replaced by a web of suspicion and paranoia.

At the personal level, the toll of unethical manipulation can be devastating. Victims may find themselves trapped in a perpetual state of confusion and self-doubt, their sense of reality distorted beyond recognition.

But the repercussions extend beyond the individual psyche. In families, workplaces, and communities, the fallout from unethical manipulation can fracture relationships. Trust, once shattered, is not easily restored, breeding resentment and animosity among those affected.

Moreover, consider the broader societal implications of unchecked manipulation. In the political arena, for instance, dark psychological tactics can be employed to sway public opinion, manipulate elections, and subvert democratic processes. The consequences of such actions reverberate through the corridors of power, eroding the very foundations of democracy.

Imagine you work in a competitive corporate environment where promotions are scarce and advancement is highly coveted. Your supervisor, let's call them Maria, is known for their Machiavellian tactics and willingness to do whatever it takes to climb the corporate ladder.

Maria regularly engages in manipulation techniques such as gaslighting, where they subtly undermine your confidence and question your competence. They might take credit for your ideas or accomplishments, leaving you feeling undervalued and powerless. Meanwhile, they nurture alliances with higher-ups by flattering and ingratiating themselves, creating a facade of loyalty and competence.

As a result, trust among colleagues begins to erode. Team dynamics become strained as everyone becomes hypervigilant, second-guessing each other's motives and actions. Productivity suffers as morale dips, and resentment simmers beneath the surface.

Outside observers may notice the toxic work environment but struggle to pinpoint the source of the discord. Meanwhile, victims of the manipulation may feel isolated and powerless, unable to speak out for fear of retaliation or further manipulation.

So, what can you do to protect yourself from the consequences of unethical manipulation? Stay vigilant. Educate yourself about the tactics being used, and be mindful of red flags in your interactions with others. Trust your instincts, and don't hesitate to seek support if you suspect you're being manipulated. By staying informed and empowered, you can cut psychological manipulation off at the knees.

Building Mental Fortitude

Mental resilience serves as both protection and a tool. It strengthens you against the devious schemes of dark psychology, enabling you to move through the complexities with clarity and power. But how do you grow and strengthen this necessary trait? It's not about brute force; it's about strategic training. Let's go through a step-by-step guide to honing your mental resilience:

- **Educate:** The first step in any battle is understanding the terrain. Educate yourself about manipulation and continue to do so. Recognize the subtle signs and patterns. Awareness serves as your early warning system, allowing you to spot manipulation before it takes root.

- **Mindfulness:** Nurture a practice of mindfulness. Train your mind to observe thoughts and emotions without judgment. By staying present in the moment, you can prevent past traumas or future anxieties from clouding your judgment. Why is this important? Manipulators will often pull vulnerable moments from your past to cause pain and take control. By staying in the here and now, you take that power back. Mindfulness builds a solid foundation for resilience, grounding you in reality.

- **Emotional regulation:** Emotions are the currency of manipulation. Learn to regulate your emotional responses not by suppressing them but by understanding them. Identify triggers and vulnerabilities. When your manipulator throws insults or names at you, don't react. Take that power away.

Practice techniques like deep breathing, meditation, or journaling to manage stress and anxiety effectively.

- **Critical thinking:** Sharpen your critical thinking skills. Question everything, especially when it seems too good to be true. Develop a healthy skepticism toward information and people. Verify facts, seek multiple perspectives, and trust your intuition. Critical thinking acts as a shield against misinformation and manipulation.

- **Boundaries:** Establish and enforce clear boundaries in your relationships and interactions. Know your limits and communicate them assertively. Boundaries serve as your frontline defense, preventing others from encroaching on your mental and emotional space. Respect yourself enough to say no when necessary.

Now, let's draw inspiration from Lily's journey.

Lily found herself entangled in a toxic marriage, where gaslighting became her husband's weapon of choice. At first, she struggled, questioning her own reality as her partner twisted the truth and undermined her confidence. She had no idea just how easy this was for him, leaning into Lily's mother's mental health issues. At any chance he got, he would hurl insults that tapped into her insecurities: "You're so unstable, just like your mother." After years of abuse and low self-esteem, Lily wanted her life back. She started looking at self-discovery and resilience-building.

Lily embraced awareness, educating herself about gaslighting and manipulation. She recognized the signs and refused to be gaslit into submission. Mindfulness became her anchor, allowing her to stay centered during the storm of confusion. She learned to regulate her emotions, refusing to let fear and doubt control her.

With a critical eye, Lily dissected the lies and half-truths woven by her partner. She reclaimed her freedom, refusing to be manipulated into submission. Boundaries became her shield, protecting her from further harm.

Today, Lily stands tall, a testament to the power of resilience. She emerged from the darkness stronger and wiser. Through her journey, she not only defended herself against psychological warfare but also inspired others to do the same. Lily's story serves as a reminder that, with resilience, we can overcome even the darkest of manipulations.

Overcoming Psychological Challenges

In the battlefield of the mind, psychological challenges can be some of the most insidious adversaries we face. When dealing with manipulation, whether through gaslighting, emotional coercion, or other dark psychological tactics, the effects can be devastating. Just remember, you have the power to overcome these challenges. It's time to reclaim your psychological sovereignty. Here's how:

- **Trust your instincts:** Gaslighting and manipulation often thrive in environments where doubt is sown. Trust your gut feelings. If something feels off or doesn't align with your sense of reality, don't dismiss it. Your intuition is a powerful defense mechanism.

- **Practice assertiveness:** Assertiveness is the antidote to manipulation. Learn to assert your needs, opinions, and boundaries with confidence and clarity. Use "I" statements to express yourself assertively while respecting the rights of others.

- **Develop emotional resilience:** Build resilience to withstand the emotional onslaught of manipulation. Nurture coping strategies such as mindfulness, deep breathing exercises, and cognitive reframing to manage stress and negative emotions effectively.

- **Continuous self-empowerment:** Overcoming psychological challenges is an ongoing process of self-empowerment. Stay vigilant, continue learning about psychology and manipulation, and refine your self-protection strategies as you evolve.

- **Harness your inner sleuth:** Become a psychological detective in your own life. Investigate the discrepancies, the inconsistencies, the subtle cues that hint at manipulation. Trust those instincts that whisper, "Something's not right here." Your intuition is your secret weapon.

- **Forge bonds of steel:** Manipulators thrive in the shadows of isolation. Don't give them that power. Surround yourself with a tribe of trusted confidants.

- **Draw the line in the sand:** Picture yourself as a fortress, fortified with boundaries of steel. Define your limits clearly and unapologetically. When someone attempts to breach those walls with manipulation, stand firm. No trespassing allowed!

- **Feed your inner flame:** Manipulation extinguishes the fire within, leaving you feeling like a flickering candle in a gusty wind. Stoke that flame with self-validation. Remind yourself of your worth, your strengths, your victories. You are the hero of your own story.

- **Sharpen your mind's blade:** Arm yourself with the weapon of critical thinking. Polish it until it gleams with the ability to cut through the fog of manipulation. Question everything, especially when it seems too good (or too bad) to be true.

- **Nourish your soul:** Your psyche is a garden, and manipulation is a weed threatening to choke the life out of it. Tend to your soul with acts of self-care. Plant seeds of joy, water them with love, and watch as resilience blooms in the face of adversity.

Post-Manipulation Coping Strategies

Once you're trapped in a place of manipulation, emerging into the light requires a strategic approach that integrates self-awareness, resilience, and proactive measures.

First, you need to acknowledge the manipulation. It's imperative to confront the reality of what you've experienced. Denial only strengthens the manipulator's grip. Ask yourself: What tactics were employed? How did they impact your thoughts and emotions?

Next, prioritize self-care. Manipulation can leave emotional scars, but nurturing your well-being is paramount. Engage in activities that replenish your spirit, whether it's meditation, exercise, or creative outlets. By nurturing yourself, you reinforce your inner strength.

Share your experience with those who validate your feelings without judgment. Discussing your ordeal with supportive individuals can provide clarity and perspective, validating your reality in the face of gaslighting.

Now, let's equip you with actionable coping strategies:

- **Maintain a journal:** Document your thoughts and emotions, allowing for introspection and self-expression. Journaling can serve as a cathartic release, enabling you to process your experiences and gain clarity.

- **Engage in grounding exercises:** Grounding techniques such as deep breathing, mindfulness, or sensory awareness can anchor you in the present moment, alleviating anxiety and restoring equilibrium.

- **Limit exposure to triggers:** Identify triggers that evoke memories of manipulation and take proactive steps to minimize exposure. Whether it's avoiding certain individuals or environments, prioritize your emotional safety.

- **Set small, achievable goals:** Break down your recovery process into manageable steps and celebrate each milestone along the way. Setting and accomplishing goals boosts your confidence and reinforces your belief in your ability to overcome challenges.

- **Practice self-compassion:** Be gentle with yourself as you move through the healing process. Recognize that recovery is a journey and setbacks are natural. Treat yourself with absolute kindness.

Remember, you possess the inner strength to transcend adversity and emerge stronger than before. Stay vigilant, stay empowered, and never underestimate the power of your own mind.

Interactive Element: The Big Picture

Recall the A.M.E.L.I.O.R.A.T.E. framework—a road map to self-protection and empowerment. Each phase of this framework serves as a step guiding you toward a deeper understanding of the psychological landscape. As we dissect the intricacies of dark psychology and gaslighting, we're not merely looking into the abyss; we're lighting the path toward resilience and self-mastery.

Consider this eighth phase of the framework. Here, we discuss resilience as a tool to healing. But knowledge alone is not enough; it's the application of this knowledge that truly empowers you.

By weaving together comprehensive insights into dark psychology with actionable self-protection strategies, we equip you with the tools to dismantle the constructs of manipulation. I challenge you to question the narratives imposed upon you, to reclaim your freedom, and to forge a reality rooted in truth and authenticity.

As we conclude this chapter on building resilience against dark psychology and gaslighting, remember that understanding the tactics of psychological manipulation is just the beginning of your journey toward empowerment. You've learned to recognize the signs, to trust your instincts, and to assert your boundaries firmly.

Looking ahead to our next chapter, we'll examine a fascinating paradox: the ethical principles that underpin our moral compass, juxtaposed against the darker shades of human behavior explored in the realm of dark psychology. Prepare to walk down a path where the boundaries between right and wrong blur as we uncover the intricate interplay between ethics and manipulation.

Chapter 9:

The Ethical Route

The human mind is both the greatest weapon and the deadliest trap. –Robert Greene

Welcome to the ninth phase of the A.M.E.L.I.O.R.A.T.E. framework: "The ethical route." It's imperative to confront the ethical considerations that accompany the world of dark psychology. Here, we explore not only the depths of human behavior but also the moral compass that guides our actions.

We need to ask ourselves: What are the ethical implications of wielding power over the minds of others? How do we reconcile the pursuit of our objectives with the principles of fairness, respect, and integrity?

In this chapter, we will confront these questions head-on, providing comprehensive insights into the ethical dilemmas inherent in the practice of dark psychology. We'll explore the psychological mechanisms behind manipulation, shedding light on the ways in which individuals can be subtly coerced, deceived, and exploited for personal gain.

Understanding Persuasion and Influence

Understanding the balance between persuasion and manipulation is pivotal, driven by the motives behind our influence and the ethical compass guiding our actions.

Renowned psychologist Robert Cialdini, through his works *Influence: The Psychology of Persuasion* and *Pre-Suasion: A Revolutionary Way to Influence and Persuade*, offers invaluable insights. Cialdini's principles, such as reciprocity, commitment, and social proof, serve as pillars of ethical persuasion. It's about presenting compelling arguments, tapping into emotions, and navigating social dynamics with integrity (Livesay, 2017).

However, manipulation often lurks in darker corners, cloaked in deceit and coercion. Unlike persuasion, manipulation sidesteps ethical boundaries, potentially sacrificing the well-being and autonomy of those under its sway. It's a place where vulnerabilities are exploited and trust is often collateral damage.

So, where do we draw the line? Ethical influence hinges on transparency, honesty, and respect for personal freedom. It's better to create connections instead of ruining them. On the other hand, manipulation depends on deceit, which breaks down trust and control.

These distinctions are vital, whether you're in the middle of marketing strategies or personal relationships. Ethical persuasion fosters trust and nurtures authentic connections, while manipulation breeds resentment and fractures bonds.

Empowerment lies in understanding persuasion's mechanics, an art I've honed keenly. Detecting manipulation becomes second nature, disarming would-be manipulators with ease. Sometimes, a simple "I'm not interested" suffices; other times, a blunt call-out exposes the ploy for what it is.

Gavin de Becker's insights into charm as a veiled form of manipulation resonate deeply. He states: "To charm is to compel, to control by allure or attraction. Think of charm as a verb, not a trait. If you consciously tell yourself, 'This person is trying to charm me' as opposed to, 'This person is charming,' you'll be able to see around it" (Joyce, 2024).

Fundamentally, the difference between manipulation and persuasion lies in ethical motives. Cialdini's principles act as guiding lights, leading us to ethical waters where comprehension and teamwork prevail. Therefore, as you skillfully utilize persuasive techniques, you can trust that your aim is always to foster authentic relationships, never to manipulate.

Positive Applications of Persuasion

Psychologists identify six characteristics of persuasion, first outlined in 1984 by Robert Cialdini, PhD, to explain the qualities that render persuasive messages effective and positive. (Alslaity & Tran, 2021). Harnessing the power of persuasion doesn't have to involve manipulation or coercion. In fact, understanding these principles can empower you to positively influence others while maintaining integrity and respect. Let's explore how you can wield these principles ethically:

- **Reciprocity:** Instead of exploiting reciprocity for personal gain, use it to foster genuine connections and goodwill. Offer help and support without expecting anything in return. By initiating acts of kindness, you set a positive precedent that encourages reciprocity naturally.

- **Scarcity:** Highlighting the scarcity of resources or opportunities can motivate action for worthy causes. For example, in fundraising efforts for a charitable organization, emphasizing limited-time donation matching can inspire people to contribute. Just ensure transparency and authenticity in your messaging to uphold trust.

- **Authority:** Position yourself as a knowledgeable and trustworthy figure by sharing expertise and valuable insights. Use your authority to educate and empower others rather than to manipulate or deceive. Remember to back your claims with credible evidence and encourage critical thinking.

- **Consistency or commitment:** Encourage positive behavior by prompting small commitments aligned with larger goals. For instance, when promoting sustainable practices, encourage individuals to start with simple actions like reducing single-use plastics. Each commitment reinforces a sense of responsibility and progress.

- **Social proof:** Highlighting collective support for virtuous causes can inspire others to join in. Share success stories, testimonials, and examples of positive impact to demonstrate the value of participation. Foster inclusive communities where individuals feel motivated by the collective effort to enact positive change.

- **Liking:** Build genuine rapport and trust with others through authentic connections. Focus on building meaningful relationships based on mutual respect and understanding. When people feel valued and appreciated, they're more receptive to collaborative efforts and constructive dialogue.

Employing these principles ethically allows you to nurture positive influence, inspire action, and contribute to meaningful change in your personal and professional endeavors.

Building Authentic Connections

What Is Empathy?

Empathy is the ability to understand and share the feelings of another. It's about putting yourself in someone else's shoes, seeing the world through their eyes, and feeling what they feel. It's a powerful tool in building genuine connections because it fosters understanding, trust, and mutual respect.

In the world of dark psychology, empathy can be manipulated and exploited. Think about it: If someone understands your emotions better than you do, they can use that knowledge to control you. They can play on your vulnerabilities, manipulate your emotions, and lead you down a path you never intended to take.

The Benefits of Empathy in Social Contexts

Empathy is needed in healthy social interactions, fostering connection, trust, and cooperation. When you genuinely empathize with others, you build rapport and strengthen relationships. It's the glue that holds communities together, creating a sense of belonging and understanding.

Being empathetic can have many benefits, including helping you feel closer and more connected to the people around you.

Builds Trust and Rapport

Empathy is like a magic key that unlocks a door to trust and understanding between people. Imagine you have a friend who really listens to you and tries to see things from your point of view. That makes you feel good, right? It's because when we take the time to understand someone's feelings, it helps them trust us more. This trust makes the bond between people stronger and communication smoother. Think of it like planting seeds of trust and watching a beautiful friendship grow.

Encourages Openness and Vulnerability

Being empathetic is like creating a safe space for others to open up and share their thoughts and feelings. Picture a cozy and warm room where your friends feel comfortable enough to share their deepest secrets and fears with you. When people feel understood, they become more willing to share their vulnerabilities. It's like offering them a reassuring hug that says, "It's okay, you can trust me." This openness is the foundation for building strong and lasting relationships with others.

Leads to More Satisfying Relationships

Empathy is the secret ingredient that makes relationships flourish. Let's say you and your friend had a misunderstanding. Instead of arguing, you try to understand why your friend feels upset. By showing empathy, you can clear up miscommunications, resolve conflicts peacefully, and strengthen your bond. This understanding leads to happier and more fulfilling connections with others. It's like adding extra sweetness to your already delicious friendship cake.

Promotes Personal Growth and Development

Empathy is like a mirror that reflects not only the feelings of others but also your own emotions. When you understand how someone else feels, it can help you understand yourself better too. This self-awareness is like a guiding light that shines on your strengths and weaknesses, helping you grow as a person. By practicing empathy, you can develop a deeper understanding of yourself and others, paving the way for personal growth and self-improvement.

Encourages Altruistic Behavior

Empathy has the power to turn you into a real-life superhero. Imagine seeing someone in need and feeling what they feel—this leads to a strong desire to help. Empathetic people are more likely to show kindness and offer support to others because they can relate to their struggles and emotions. It's like having a superhero cape made of kindness and understanding that inspires you to make the world a better place, one empathetic act at a time.

Increases Happiness and Well-Being

Have you ever noticed how good it feels to help someone in need? That warm and fuzzy feeling of making a positive impact on someone's life is what empathy is all about. Empathetic people experience higher levels of happiness and well-being because they connect with others on a deeper level. By understanding and sharing the joys and sorrows of those around them, they create a sense of belonging and fulfillment that brings joy to their own hearts.

Empathy is not just a word; it's a superpower that has the potential to transform relationships, personal growth, and the world around us. By practicing empathy in our daily lives, we can build stronger connections, foster personal development, and spread kindness and compassion wherever we go. So, let's embrace the power of empathy and make the world a brighter and more understanding place for us all.

How to Nurture Empathy

Empathy is more than a soft skill; it's a powerful tool in your tool kit for handling the complexities of human interactions. It has the ability to transform relationships, enhance well-being, and solidify connections with others. However, do not be deceived. Empathy is not solely an inherent quality—it is a skill that can be developed and employed effectively. Some may possess a natural inclination toward empathy, but for others, it's a muscle waiting to be flexed and strengthened. Here's your tactical guide to becoming an empathy powerhouse:

- **Decode nonverbal signals:** When engaging with others, decrypt their body language and subtle cues. These silent messengers unveil the emotions and thoughts brewing beneath the surface, providing invaluable intel for understanding their inner world.

- **Penetrate their perspective:** True empathy begins with stepping into someone else's shoes, seeing through their eyes, and feeling with their heart. Ask yourself: What would it be like to walk in their reality? How would their emotions resonate within you? This helps you unlock the door to genuine connection.

- **Engage in active reconnaissance:** Active listening isn't just hearing words; it's dissecting emotions, dissecting intentions, and dissecting vulnerabilities. Dive deep into their narrative, absorbing every nuance, every inflection, and every unsaid word.

- **Deploy authentic understanding:** Once you've penetrated their emotional fortress, express your comprehension with precision. Show them you're not just an observer but a fellow traveler in the labyrinth of their emotions. Avoid the pitfall of comparing or minimizing; instead, validate their experience with unwavering sincerity.

- **Neutralize assumptions:** In the fog of empathy, assumptions are your greatest adversary. Refrain from projecting your thoughts onto their canvas. Instead, look with curiosity, asking probing questions to light the way to genuine understanding.

- **Defend against bias:** Beware the shadows of bias lurking within your psyche. Recognize your predispositions and prejudices, for they distort the lens through which you perceive others. Purge them from your arsenal, allowing clarity to reign supreme.

- **Sharpen your empathetic blade:** Empathy is not a one-time conquest; it's a lifelong crusade. Arm yourself with opportunities to refine your skills. Volunteer for causes close to your heart, engage with diverse voices, and cultivate a heightened awareness of emotions—both yours and those of others around you.

When we balance human interaction, empathy emerges as the hero. Master its intricacies, wield it with skill, and watch as it changes not only your relationships but the very fabric of your existence.

Harnessing the Power of Positive Psychology

What exactly is positive psychology? It's the scientific blueprint for crafting a life that's about not just surviving but thriving. Think about it as a methodical approach to understanding what makes life truly worth living. Instead of dwelling on weaknesses, positive psychology shines a light on strengths. It's about constructing the good in life rather than patching up the bad.

Now, let's break down what positive psychology entails. It explores levels of positive experiences like happiness and love, positive states and traits such as gratitude and resilience, and even positive institutions—think of applying these principles within entire organizations. It's a holistic approach, examining the entirety of human experience through a lens of growth, strength, and possibility.

Let's uncover what positive psychology means for you. It's not merely a fluffy concept; it's a game changer in the landscape of mental health. Unlike traditional psychology, which often fixates on weaknesses and pathology, positive psychology shifts the focus to strengths and resilience. It's about building a life that's not just okay but exceptional.

Positive psychology isn't a passing fad; it's a revolutionary shift in how we perceive mental health. It was Martin Seligman who laid the groundwork back in 2000, challenging the status quo and championing a psychology of possibility. Seligman's vision was clear: to create a field that didn't just heal wounds but nurtured strengths (Ackerman, 2024).

But what are the core principles of positive psychology? At its essence, positive psychology revolves around the PERMA model: positive emotions, engagement, relationships, meaning, and accomplishment. These aren't just abstract concepts; they're the building blocks of a life well-lived. By honing these elements, individuals can cultivate resilience, find purpose, and navigate life's challenges with grace.

Positive psychology isn't a replacement for traditional therapy; it's a powerful complement. It's about celebrating what's right with you rather than dwelling on what's wrong. It's about forging a path toward a life that's not just good but extraordinary.

Utilizing Positive Psychology in Everyday Life

Let's get practical. How can you harness the principles of positive psychology in your everyday life, turning theory into tangible action? Here's a road map:

- **Embrace gratitude:** Start each day by reflecting on what you're grateful for. It could be as simple as a warm cup of coffee or a supportive friend. Cultivating gratitude shifts your focus from scarcity to abundance, fostering a mindset of appreciation and contentment.

- **Find meaningful engagement:** Identify activities that truly engage you. Whether it's painting, gardening, or volunteering, immerse yourself in pursuits that ignite your passion. By engaging fully in these activities, you not only experience joy in the moment but also cultivate a sense of purpose and fulfillment.

- **Nurture relationships:** Invest time and energy in nurturing meaningful connections with others. Reach out to friends and family, schedule regular catch-ups, and prioritize quality time together. Strong social bonds not only boost your mood but also serve as a buffer against life's challenges.

- **Seek meaning:** Reflect on what gives your life meaning and purpose. It could be pursuing a career that aligns with your values, volunteering for a cause you're passionate about, or nurturing relationships with loved ones. When you have a sense of purpose, even the toughest obstacles become more manageable.

- **Celebrate achievements:** Take time to acknowledge and celebrate your accomplishments, no matter how small. Whether it's completing a project at work or reaching a personal milestone, recognize your efforts and the progress you've made. Celebrating achievements boosts self-esteem and motivates you to continue striving for success.

- **Practice self-compassion:** Be kind to yourself, especially during challenging times. Treat yourself with the same compassion and understanding that you would offer to a friend facing difficulties. Practice self-care activities that nourish your body, mind, and soul, whether it's meditation, exercise, or spending time in nature.

- **Challenge negative thoughts:** Pay attention to your inner dialogue and challenge negative thoughts as they arise. Replace self-criticism with self-compassion and self-empowerment. Reframe setbacks as opportunities for growth and learning rather than insurmountable obstacles.

- **Cultivate optimism:** Foster a mindset of optimism and hope, even in the face of adversity. Focus on what you can control and take proactive steps toward positive change. Nourish resilience by viewing challenges as temporary setbacks rather than permanent failures.

When you integrate these practices into your daily routine, you'll not only enhance your mental well-being but also nurture a life filled with purpose, meaning, and joy. Remember, positive psychology isn't just a theory—it's a blueprint for living your best life.

Creating Win–Win Situations Through Ethical Influence

Okay, let's explore the world of ethical influence, a potent strategy for maneuvering through the complex place of psychological persuasion with honesty. How can you leverage this ability to safeguard yourself and also establish mutually beneficial outcomes in your interactions? Here's what you need to know:

- **Empathize with others:** Utilize empathy skills and put yourself in the shoes of those you seek to influence. Understand their needs, desires, and concerns. Demonstrate genuine care and concern, laying the groundwork for effective communication and collaboration.

- **Focus on win–win outcomes**: Shift your mindset from zero-sum games to win–win solutions. Seek outcomes that benefit all parties involved rather than prioritizing your own interests at the expense of others. Win–win situations foster goodwill and cooperation, paving the way for long-term success.

- **Utilize persuasive communication:** Master the art of persuasive communication to ethically influence others. Clearly articulate your ideas, listen actively to the perspectives of others, and find common ground for collaboration. Effective communication builds rapport and fosters mutual understanding—essential ingredients for ethical influence.

- **Lead by example:** Lead by example and embody the principles of ethical influence in your own behavior. Demonstrate integrity, fairness, and respect in all your interactions, serving as a role model for others to follow. Your actions speak louder than words, shaping the culture of trust and cooperation within your social circle.

- **Be open to feedback:** Remain open to feedback and constructive criticism from others. Use feedback as an opportunity for growth and self-improvement, refining your approach to ethical influence over time. Continuous learning and adaptation are key to mastering this skill and maximizing its impact.

- **Stay mindful of power dynamics:** Be mindful of power dynamics in your interactions and strive to balance power relations ethically. Avoid exploiting your influence for personal gain or manipulating others to achieve your objectives. Ethical influence is rooted in respect for autonomy and fairness, regardless of relative power.

Ethical influence involves fostering collaboration, building trust, and creating win–win outcomes for all parties involved. So, go forth with confidence, armed with the power of ethical influence to shape positive outcomes and forge meaningful connections in your personal and professional life.

Interactive Element: The Big Picture

Let's circle back to the essence of the A.M.E.L.I.O.R.A.T.E. framework. It's not just a series of steps; it's a comprehensive strategy for fortifying your defenses and navigating the complexities of psychological warfare. Each phase serves a distinct purpose, and here we are at the end of the ninth phase: "The ethical route."

So, how does this connect to the broader mission of the A.M.E.L.I.O.R.A.T.E. framework? Consider it a large piece of the puzzle. By integrating the insights gleaned from our exploration of dark psychology, you elevate your understanding of human nature to new heights. You become not just a passive observer but an active participant in the understanding of ethics and morality.

Remember that true power lies not in manipulation but in understanding and compassion. By wielding your knowledge responsibly and ethically, you elevate yourself above the machinations of deceit and emerge as a light of authenticity and integrity.

This chapter serves as a crucial piece in your quest for mastery over the nuances of psychological warfare. With each insight gleaned and each strategy honed, you edge closer to unlocking the secrets of the human psyche and harnessing its potential for positive change.

In the next chapter, we will explore the fascinating world of neurolinguistic programming (NLP), unveiling the profound ways in which language shapes our thoughts, behaviors, and perceptions.

Chapter 10:

Exploring Neurolinguistic Programming

Getting control of someone's mind is easy. But keeping in touch with that mind with the correct use of words is difficult enough. –Unknown

As we begin the final leg of our expedition within the realm of the human psyche, we uncover the profound intricacies of NLP. Within these pages lies the key to unlocking the hidden patterns of thought and behavior that shape our reality, both internally and externally.

As we navigate the terrain of NLP in this final phase of the A.M.E.L.I.O.R.A.T.E. framework, we will unravel its mysteries, dissect its principles, and explore its practical applications. You will emerge from these pages with a profound understanding of NLP and its implications for your life.

Understanding Neurolinguistic Programming

Neurolinguistic programming, often abbreviated as NLP, is like getting a backstage pass to your brain. It's all about figuring out how your brain works and using that knowledge to take control of your life. Imagine your brain as a complex machine with different parts: the hardware (neurology), the language you use (linguistics), and the software that runs the whole show (programming).

Think of neurology as the wiring in your brain. It involves everything from your physical nerves to your thoughts and emotions. It's like your brain's electrical system, connecting everything together. When you understand this, you can start to see how your thoughts and feelings are all connected, influencing your actions and decisions.

Language is how you communicate, not just with others but with yourself. It's the link between your inner thoughts and the outside world. The words you use shape how you see things and how others see you. By understanding the power of language, you can change how you perceive yourself and others, leading to better interactions and relationships.

Your brain is like a powerful computer, constantly running programs based on your past experiences, beliefs, and emotions. These programs dictate how you act and react to different situations. By learning about NLP, you're essentially getting the manual to your brain's operating system. You can tweak the settings, uninstall old programs (habits), and install new ones that serve you better.

The Unconscious Mind: Your Ally in Disguise

Your unconscious mind is like a loyal but sometimes misunderstood friend. It works hard to bring you what it thinks you want, even if it's not what you consciously desire. Imagine it as a waiter in a restaurant— it will keep serving you procrastination, anxiety, and emotional baggage unless you clearly tell it what you actually want to order instead.

When you grasp the concepts of NLP, you essentially learn to speak the language of your unconscious mind. It's like having a heart-to-heart chat with a close friend who wants to help you achieve your goals. By communicating clearly with your subconscious, you can guide it toward what you truly desire, setting the stage for positive outcomes and personal growth.

Language as a Tool of Manipulation

Manipulators use words to influence others. They carefully pick words to make others do what they want. They might make things sound better or worse than they really are. This helps them control how people feel and act. They want people to believe them and do what they say.

Tricking With Words

Manipulators have a way of using words to influence how others perceive the world around them. This can involve tactics such as casting doubt on people's beliefs or emotions. Sometimes, they resort to falsehoods or distorting facts to sow seeds of uncertainty in the minds of their targets. Consequently, those people find themselves in a state of confusion and hesitation regarding the authenticity of their perceptions and realities.

When someone manipulates with words, they may attempt to alter the way others view certain situations or concepts. For instance, they could present a scenario in a different light, causing people to question their initial understanding of the matter. By doing so, the manipulator creates a sense of ambiguity and disbelief, leading the other party to wonder if their original standpoint was accurate.

Manipulators often resort to lies and half-truths to instill a sense of uncertainty in their targets. They may deliberately distort the truth or omit vital information, leaving others in a state of confusion. The resulting uncertainty can be disorienting, causing individuals to second-guess their perceptions and interpretations of events.

One common aim of manipulators is to instigate self-doubt in their victims. By using words to challenge the beliefs and feelings of others, they can erode their confidence and trust in themselves. This manipulation tactic can lead individuals to question their judgment, their feelings, and even their sense of reality, fostering a sense of insecurity and hesitation.

Changing What Words Mean

Manipulators change the meanings of words to suit their needs. They might use words that are not clear or switch between two meanings. This confuses others and makes it hard for them to understand what's really going on. By doing this, manipulators can take advantage of others without them knowing.

Creating a Secret Language

In groups where manipulation happens, there might be special words only group members use. This makes people in the group feel like they belong somewhere unique. By having their own language, manipulators control how their followers think and act. This keeps them tied to the group's beliefs.

Messages You Don't Notice

Manipulators can send messages without you realizing it. They might use their tone of voice or body language to make you feel a certain way. They could also hide messages in what they say or write. These hidden messages can make you do things without knowing why.

Knowing how manipulators use language is essential. By understanding their tricks, you can guard against being controlled. Stay aware of these tactics to maintain your independence and make your own choices in interactions.

Empowerment Through Awareness

Awareness of manipulative tactics and their potential impact is a key aspect of safeguarding yourself against deceptive language. By educating yourself on common manipulation strategies and red flags, you can enhance your ability to detect and resist attempts at psychological influence. This knowledge empowers you to maintain autonomy and self-assurance in the face of manipulative language.

Applying NLP in Psychological Manipulation

NLP is a psychological tool that explores the complex interplay among language, behavior, and neurological functions to exert control over others. By grasping and utilizing NLP methods, you can influence perceptions subtly, manage emotions, and steer outcomes to protect yourself.

Let's delve into some NLP techniques for influencing others:

- **Mirroring and matching:** People are naturally drawn to those who reflect their own behavior and mannerisms. By subtly mirroring someone's gestures, posture, speech patterns, and even breathing, they can establish rapport and gain your trust effortlessly. Pay attention to their body language, tone of voice, and choice of words, and remain aware.

- **Pacing and leading:** Manipulators will begin by pacing your current reality, acknowledging your thoughts and feelings without judgment. Once rapport is established, they will gradually introduce suggestions or ideas that lead you toward their desired outcome. This technique capitalizes on the principle of unconscious influence, where subtle shifts in language and tone can guide you toward a predetermined conclusion.

- **Anchoring:** Our brains associate certain emotions with specific stimuli. By creating anchors—repeatedly pairing a particular gesture, word, or image with a desired emotional state— manipulators trigger that emotion at will. For example, if they want to appear confident in your presence, they will consistently associate a specific hand gesture or phrase with feelings of confidence during your interactions.

- **Embedded commands:** These are subtle directives hidden within ordinary speech. Manipulators will emphasize certain words or phrases and subtly alter their tone, planting suggestions in your subconscious mind without your awareness. For instance, saying "As you relax and consider my proposal, you'll find yourself more inclined to agree" subtly nudges you toward compliance while maintaining the facade of a casual conversation.

- **Utilization:** This technique involves adapting to and leveraging your responses in real time. Instead of rigidly sticking to a predefined script, remain flexible and responsive to their cues. When they incorporate and validate your input, they establish a sense of collaboration and cooperation, making you more receptive to their influence.

When you understand and master these NLP techniques for influence and adopt proactive self-protection strategies, you can move through the intricate landscape of psychological manipulation with confidence and resilience.

Manipulating Thoughts and Behaviors With NLP

NLP operates on the premise that our thoughts, emotions, and behaviors are interconnected, and that by altering one aspect we can influence the others. Here's how thoughts and behaviors can be manipulated through the cunning application of NLP techniques:

- **Language patterns:** Words have power. By carefully selecting language that evokes specific emotions or associations, manipulators can subtly shape your thoughts and perceptions. They may employ persuasive language patterns, such as using positive framing to encourage compliance or negative framing to instill fear or doubt.

- **Reframing:** Manipulators adept in NLP can refract your reality, altering the meaning of events or situations to serve their agenda. By reframing your interpretation of past experiences or current circumstances, they can manipulate your emotions and behaviors. For example, they may reinterpret criticism as constructive feedback to maintain control over your self-esteem and decision-making.

- **Submodalities:** NLP explores the nuances of sensory experiences, known as submodalities, to influence perceptions and responses. Manipulators may exploit submodalities to amplify or diminish the impact of certain stimuli on your thoughts and behaviors. Manipulating visual imagery, auditory cues, or kinesthetic sensations allows them to elicit specific emotional responses or trigger desired behaviors.

- **Anchoring and triggering:** Through repeated association of specific stimuli with certain emotions or behaviors, manipulators can create powerful anchors in your psyche. These anchors act as triggers, activating predetermined responses without conscious awareness. Whether it's a particular word, gesture, or environmental cue, these triggers can be exploited to manipulate your thoughts and behaviors in predictable ways.

- **Sensory rich language:** NLP emphasizes the use of sensory-rich language to create vivid mental imagery and evoke visceral responses. Manipulators skillfully craft their communication to engage your senses, intensifying emotional arousal and influencing your cognitive processes. When they appeal to your sensory perceptions, they can implant suggestions or directives that shape your thoughts and behaviors without being detected.

Now, armed with this understanding, let's explore actionable self-protection strategies to safeguard your mind against manipulation:

- **Develop critical thinking skills:** Foster a discerning mindset that questions information, evaluates motives, and analyzes the implications of persuasive tactics. Train yourself to spot inconsistencies, logical fallacies, and emotional manipulation techniques.

- **Enhance emotional intelligence:** Heighten your self-awareness and emotional resilience to recognize and regulate your own emotions. Understanding your emotional triggers and vulnerabilities can help you fortify yourself against manipulative influence and maintain emotional equilibrium.

- **Set boundaries:** Establish clear boundaries in your relationships and interactions to protect your autonomy and well-being. Communicate assertively and enforce consequences for violations of your boundaries, refusing to yield to manipulation or coercion.

- **Strengthen self-confidence:** Nurture a strong sense of self-worth and confidence in your abilities. Manipulators often prey on insecurities and self-doubt, so bolstering your self-esteem can render you less susceptible to their tactics.

- **Seek support:** Surround yourself with trusted allies who have your best interests at heart. Share your concerns and experiences with supportive people who can offer perspective, validation, and encouragement in challenging situations.

Ethical Considerations in NLP Mind Control

Let's delve into the ethical considerations surrounding the use of NLP techniques in mind control. While NLP can be a tool for influencing thoughts and behaviors, its application raises profound questions about morality and responsibility. Here's how you can wield NLP techniques responsibly:

- **Informed consent:** Respect the autonomy and agency of others by obtaining their informed consent before employing NLP techniques. Transparently communicate your intentions and the potential impact of your influence, allowing them to make an informed decision about their participation.

- **Empowerment, not manipulation:** Shift your focus from manipulation to empowerment. Instead of coercing or controlling others for personal gain, empower them to make autonomous choices aligned with their values and aspirations. Use NLP techniques to facilitate self-awareness, growth, and positive change rather than exploitation.

- **Alignment with ethical principles:** Align your use of NLP techniques with ethical principles such as beneficence, non-maleficence, justice, and respect for autonomy. Consider the broader ethical implications of your actions and strive to uphold the dignity and well-being of all those involved.

- **Integrity and transparency:** Maintain integrity and transparency in your communication and interactions. Be honest about your intentions and avoid deceptive or manipulative tactics that undermine trust and integrity. Build authentic connections based on mutual respect and transparency.

- **Ethical reflection and accountability:** Engage in ongoing ethical reflection and self-examination to evaluate the ethical implications of your use of NLP techniques. Take responsibility for the consequences of your actions and be willing to course-correct if you veer into ethically dubious territory.

Balancing Influence and Respect for Autonomy

Let's explore the intricate balance required in using influence while also honoring the independence of others within the realm of psychological manipulation. As we navigate this complex landscape, it's crucial to keep in mind the primary aim of this endeavor: to equip ourselves and those around us with profound insights into psychological tactics while maintaining ethical standards and a genuine respect for human dignity:

- **Understanding the dynamics of influence:** Influence is a natural aspect of human interaction. Whether through subtle persuasion or overt coercion, we all seek to influence others to some extent. However, the key lies in understanding the ethical boundaries and responsible use of influence. By recognizing the power dynamics at play, we can navigate influence with sensitivity and awareness.

- **Respecting autonomy:** Autonomy encompasses the right to self-determination, independent thought, and freedom of choice. Respecting the autonomy of others means honoring their agency and allowing them to make decisions aligned with their own values and interests, free from undue influence or manipulation.

- **Empowerment through consent:** True empowerment arises from informed consent and voluntary participation. When seeking to influence others, prioritize transparency and communication. Offer information openly, encourage dialogue, and invite active participation. By respecting others' autonomy and providing them with the knowledge and agency to make informed choices, we empower them to engage with us authentically and willingly.

- **Building genuine connections:** Authentic influence emerges from genuine connections built on mutual trust, respect, and understanding. Instead of resorting to manipulation tactics, focus on fostering meaningful relationships grounded in empathy and authenticity. By prioritizing empathy and actively listening to others' perspectives, we demonstrate respect for their autonomy and cultivate rapport based on mutual respect.

- **Navigating power dynamics:** Acknowledge and address power differentials that may impact the balance of influence and autonomy in relationships. Whether in professional settings, interpersonal dynamics, or broader societal contexts, be mindful of the inherent power dynamics at play and strive to mitigate disparities through equitable communication, active listening, and inclusive decision-making processes.

- **Maintaining ethical integrity:** Uphold ethical integrity as a guiding principle in all interactions. Recognize the inherent dignity and worth of every individual, and refrain from exploiting vulnerabilities or resorting to manipulation tactics that undermine autonomy or cause harm. Commit to ethical reflection and accountability, and be willing to course-correct if your actions veer into ethically dubious territory.

Navigating the interplay between influence and respect for autonomy with mindfulness and integrity allows you to foster healthier, more equitable relationships and contribute to a more ethical and compassionate world. Remember, true empowerment arises from honoring the autonomy and dignity of others while wielding influence responsibly and ethically.

Interactive Element: The Big Picture

As we finalize this chapter, let's recall the overarching A.M.E.L.I.O.R.A.T.E. framework, a guide through the intricate terrain of self-protection and psychological empowerment. This framework is a path toward a deeper comprehension of psychological warfare and practical strategies for defense.

This final phase of the framework, exploring NLP, explored unlocking the language of the mind—the locked patterns of thought and behavior that shape our reality. Be mindful that this isn't just about defense; it's about reclaiming your narrative, asserting your truth, and forging a path toward empowerment and liberation.

Now, as we bid adieu to this chapter and our journey through the realms of psychological warfare, remember this: Understanding NLP isn't just about defense; it's about reclaiming your power and rewriting the script of your life. By decoding the subtle nuances of communication, you unlock the key to authentic self-expression and unshakeable confidence.

Conclusion

As we conclude this voyage through the complex maze of dark psychology and gaslighting, it's a moment to contemplate the journey we've undertaken and the resources we've acquired on this path. Utilizing the A.M.E.L.I.O.R.A.T.E. framework, we have maneuvered through the obscure realms of manipulation and surfaced equipped with knowledge, insight, and strength.

- **Accessing dark psychology:** We began by peeling back the layers of dark psychology, understanding its origins, evolution, and manifestations in our daily lives. By shedding light on the shadows, we empowered ourselves to recognize the subtle cues and tactics employed by those who seek to manipulate.

- **Manipulation—core concepts in psychology:** Armed with a deeper understanding of manipulation, we dissected its core concepts, dissecting its mechanisms and unraveling its mysteries. By grasping the psychology behind manipulation, we gained a foothold in the battle for our own autonomy.

- **Exploring the techniques road map:** We began exploring the realm of psychological methods, breaking down strategies and tactics with precision. By charting the landscape of influence, we armed ourselves with the instruments needed to traverse its dangerous territory.

- **Leading covert techniques in dark psychology:** We delved into the shadows, exploring covert tactics and ethical considerations. By shining a light on the darkness, we learned to distinguish between manipulation and genuine connection.

- **Introducing self-protection:** We fortified ourselves with tactics and tips for self-protection, erecting barriers against manipulation and safeguarding our mental well-being. By prioritizing self-care, we became our own guardians in the face of adversity.

- **Overtures of gaslighting:** We confronted the silent weapon of gaslighting, dissecting its insidious nature and its profound impact on our psyche. By exposing the truth, we reclaimed our reality and shattered the illusions cast upon us.

- **Reframing your tool kit for psychological warfare:** Armed with every tool in our arsenal, we stood ready to wage war against psychological manipulation. By harnessing our knowledge and deploying it ethically, we emerged as warriors of the mind, champions of truth and integrity.

- **Accessing resilience post-manipulation:** For those who have faced manipulation, this chapter served as a source of hope, guiding you on the path to recovery and resilience. By embracing positivity and self-love, we rose from the ashes, stronger than before.

- **The ethical route:** We trod the delicate balance between manipulation and ethics, forging a path that honored our principles and values. By choosing the ethical route, we created strategies that uplift rather than harm.

- **Exploring NLP:** We peered into the realm of NLP, unlocking its potential and understanding its impact on dark psychology. By harnessing the power of NLP, we gained insight into the inner workings of the mind, empowering ourselves to navigate the twists and turns of human behavior.

As we stand on the precipice of transformation, let us not forget that we are all susceptible to the siren call of dark psychology. But armed with knowledge, awareness, and resilience, we need not succumb to its allure. Let us write our own success story, one of empowerment, enlightenment, and liberation from the shackles of manipulation.

As you close this book, I ask you to reflect on the insights you've gained. If this book has helped you in any way, I urge you to share your thoughts and experiences. Your review could lead this book into the hands of those who need it most.

We can pave the way for a future free from the shadows of manipulation and gaslighting. For in knowledge and awareness lies the power to reclaim our autonomy and rewrite our destiny.

With gratitude.

References

About covert emotional manipulation. (n.d.). Psychopaths and Love. https://psychopathsandlove.com/covert-emotional-manipulation/

Ackerman, C. E. (2024, March 13). *What is positive psychology & why is it important?* PositivePsychology.com. https://positivepsychology.com/what-is-positive-psychology-definition/

Alslaity, A., & Tran, T. (2021). Users' responsiveness to persuasive techniques in recommender systems. *Frontiers in Artificial Intelligence, 4*(2). https://doi.org/10.3389/frai.2021.679459

Bhair, S. (2020, July 6). *Dark psychology—science of manipulation.* Medium. https://medium.com/@shradhabhair/dark-psychology-science-of-manipulation-1eb95ae749b3

Buffalmano, L. (n.d.-a). *Manipulation: Techniques, strategies, and ethics.* The Power Moves. https://thepowermoves.com/manipulation/

Buffalmano, L. (n.d.-b). *30 covert emotional manipulation tactics: Summary and review.* The Power Moves. https://thepowermoves.com/30-covert-emotional-manipulation-tactics/

Camacho, N. A. (2022, February 15). 8 gaslighting tactics to know about so you can protect yourself from dangerous manipulation. Well+Good. https://www.wellandgood.com/gaslighting-tactics/

Chandler, D. (2008, October 21). *Tuning in to unconscious communication.* MIT News, Massachusetts Institute of Technology. https://news.mit.edu/2008/signals-1021

Cherry, K. (2023a, July 25). *Anna Freud biography (1895-1982)*. Verywell Mind; Verywell Mind. https://www.verywellmind.com/anna-freud-biography-1895-1982-2795536

Cherry, K. (2023b, November 13). *The Asch conformity experiments*. Verywell Mind. https://www.verywellmind.com/the-asch-conformity-experiments-2794996

Cherry, K. (2023c, November 13). *How persuasion impacts us every day*. Verywell Mind. https://www.verywellmind.com/what-is-persuasion-2795892

Cherry, K. (2024, March 6). *20 defense mechanisms we use to protect ourselves*. Verywell Mind. https://www.verywellmind.com/defense-mechanisms-2795960

Coercive control: 10 signs it's gaslighting. (2019, May 15). Grampian Women's Aid. https://www.grampian-womens-aid.com/newsevents/gaslighting-10-signs/

Cramer, P. (2015). Understanding defense mechanisms. *Psychodynamic Psychiatry*, *43*(4), 523–552. https://doi.org/10.1521/pdps.2015.43.4.523

Delgado, J. (2020, November 3). *Verbal manipulation: When you hurt someone to control him*. Psychology Spot. https://psychology-spot.com/verbal-manipulation/

Depow, G. J., Francis, Z., & Inzlicht, M. (2021). The experience of empathy in everyday life. *Psychological Science*, *32*(8), 1198–1213. https://doi.org/10.1177/0956797621995202

Dexter, G. (2023, June 15). *Signs of manipulative behavior*. Verywell Health. https://www.verywellhealth.com/manipulative-behavior-5214329

The difference between persuasion & manipulation. (n.d.). Hoffeld Group. https://www.hoffeldgroup.com/the-difference-between-persuasion-manipulation/

Dr. Sanjay. (2023, July 17). *Dark psychology* [Image attached] [Post]. LinkedIn. https://www.linkedin.com/pulse/dark-psychology-exposing-now/

Dr. Weber. (2019, October 27). *5 basic body language signals of manipulators.* Dr. Weber Coaching. https://drwebercoaching.com/5-basic-body-language-signals-of-manipulators/

Friedman, W. J. (2011, June 24). *Developing an inner meter on manipulation—a critical life skill* . MentalHelp.net. https://www.mentalhelp.net/blogs/developing-an-inner-meter-on-manipulation-a-critical-life-skill/

Gaslighting widespread in the UK workplace. (2019, April 1). MHR. https://mhrglobal.com/uk/en/knowledge-hub/hr/gaslighting-widespread-uk-workplace

Geden, M., Smith, A., Campbell, J., Spain, R., Amos-Binks, A., Mott, B., Feng, J., & Lester, J. (2019). Construction and validation of an anticipatory thinking assessment. *Frontiers in Psychology, 10*, 1–2. https://doi.org/10.3389/fpsyg.2019.02749

Godden, J. (2008, July 26). *Dorpat, Paul (b. 1938).* HistoryLink.org. https://www.historylink.org/file/8704

Greenwald, G. (2014, February 24). *How covert agents infiltrate the internet to manipulate, deceive, and destroy reputations.* The Intercept. https://theintercept.com/2014/02/24/jtrig-manipulation/

Hoberman, J. (2019, August 23). Why "gaslight" hasn't lost its glow. *The New York Times.* https://www.nytimes.com/2019/08/21/arts/gaslight-movie-afterlife.html

Huizen, J. (2024, March 22). *Examples and signs of gaslighting and how to respond.* Medical News Today. https://www.medicalnewstoday.com/articles/gaslighting

James, M. (n.d.). *What is NLP?* NLP Training. https://www.nlp.com/what-is-nlp/

Jones, J. (n.d.). *Dark psychology & manipulation: Are you unknowingly using them?* Dr Jason Jones. https://drjasonjones.com/dark_psychology/

Joyce, C. (2024, January 18). *Persuasion v. manipulation* [Image attached] [Post]. LinkedIn. https://www.linkedin.com/pulse/persuasion-v-manipulation-chip-joyce-ccp-1wqoe/

Karakurt, G., & Silver, K. E. (2013). Emotional abuse in intimate relationships: the role of gender and age. *Violence and Victims, 28*(5), 804–821. https://doi.org/10.1891/0886-6708.vv-d-12-00041

Kimbrough, S. (2023, July 18). *Overt and covert abuse: What is the difference?* Marriage Recovery Center. https://marriagerecoverycenter.com/overt-and-covert-abuse/

Kueche, R. (2023, September 19). *The effects of gaslighting on mental health.* Harbor Psychiatry & Mental Health. https://harbormentalhealth.com/2023/09/19/the-effects-of-gaslighting-on-mental-health/

Lindner, J. (2023, December 20). *Must-know gaslighting statistics.* Gitnux. https://gitnux.org/gaslighting-statistics/

Livesay, J. (2017, January 18). *Pre-suasion: A revolutionary way to influence and persuade – Dr. Robert Cialdini* [Image attached] [Post]. LinkedIn. https://www.linkedin.com/pulse/pre-suasion-revolutionary-way-influence-persuade-dr-robert-livesay/

Logue, J. (2018, October 24). *The power of psychological warfare in World War II*. SAGU. https://www.sagu.edu/thoughthub/logue/

Machiavelli, N. (n.d.). *Niccolo Machiavelli quotes*. BrainyQuote. https://www.brainyquote.com/authors/niccolo-machiavelli-quotes

Main, P. (2023, May 3). *The Stanley Milgram experiment: Understanding obedience*. Structural Learning. https://www.structural-learning.com/post/stanley-milgram-experiment

Mandal, E., & Kocur, D. (2013). The Machiavellianism and manipulation tactics used by patients with borderline personality disorder in everyday life and in therapy. *Psychiatria Polska, 47*(4), 667–678. https://pubmed.ncbi.nlm.nih.gov/24946473/

Martínez, N., Connelly, C., Perez, A., & Calero, P. (2021). Self-care: A concept analysis. *International Journal of Nursing Sciences, 8*(4), 418–425. https://doi.org/10.1016/j.ijnss.2021.08.007

Maybray, B. (2023, September 6). *Gaslighting at work: How to identify it and 5 ways to address it*. HubSpot. https://blog.hubspot.com/marketing/gaslighting-at-work

Mayo Clinic Staff. (2023, December 23). *Resilience: Build skills to endure hardship*. Mayo Clinic. https://www.mayoclinic.org/tests-procedures/resilience-training/in-depth/resilience/art-20046311

McCormick, M. (n.d.). *Immanuel Kant: Metaphysics*. Internet Encyclopedia of Philosophy. https://iep.utm.edu/kantmeta/

Mcleod, S. (2023, November 17). *Stanford prison experiment: Zimbardo's famous study*. Simply Psychology. https://www.simplypsychology.org/zimbardo.html

Mirza, N. (2023, October 27). *The silent battle: Psychological warfare and its impact on common people* [Image attached] [Post]. LinkedIn. https://www.linkedin.com/pulse/silent-battle-psychological-warfare-its-impact-common-mirza-diyof/

Murray, R. (2016, November 8). *Five tips for nurturing your emotional intelligence.* Robert Murray. https://robert-murray.com/nurturing-emotional-intelligence/

Nasser, K. (2020, December 13). *Toxic manipulative communication: Avoid these traps.* Kate Nasser. https://katenasser.com/toxic-manipulative-communication-avoid-these-traps-people-skills/

Ni, P. (2015, October 11). *14 signs of psychological and emotional manipulation.* Psychology Today. https://www.psychologytoday.com/ca/blog/communication-success/201510/14-signs-psychological-and-emotional-manipulation

Overt vs. covert behavior (relationship examples). (2023, January 19). The Mend Project. https://themendproject.com/overt-vs-covert-behavior-examples/

Panchal, R. (2023, September 25). *350+ dark psychology quotes: Insightful perspectives.* Leader Boy. https://theleaderboy.com/dark-psychology-quotes/

Pedersen, T. (2022, April 28).*What are triggers, and how do they form?* Psych Central. https://psychcentral.com/lib/what-is-a-trigger

Petty, A. (2018, February 23). *11 principles of positive persuasion for workplace conversations.* Management Excellence by Art Petty. https://artpetty.com/2018/02/23/positive-persuasion-workplace-conversations/

Positive psychology principles: What they are and how they can help your mental health. (2023, June 23). Telemynd.

https://mytime.telemynd.com/telemyndblog/positive-psychology-principles-what-they-are-and-how-they-can-help-your-mental-health/

Regan, S. (2023, June 22). *Are you manipulative? 13 behaviors to watch for in yourself.* Mindbodygreen. https://www.mindbodygreen.com/articles/am-i-manipulative

Rou, C. (2023, October 20). *Navigate the mind maze: Essential NLP techniques for mental health professionals.* Quenza. https://quenza.com/blog/knowledge-base/nlp-techniques-/

Sayid, A. (2022, December 28). *Let the buyer beware: Caveat emptor* [Image attached] [Post]. LinkedIn. https://www.linkedin.com/pulse/let-buyer-beware-caveat-emptor-aamir-sayid/

Simon, G. (2022, September 22). *Manipulation and gaslighting early research.* Character Matters. https://www.drgeorgesimon.com/manipulation-and-gaslighting-early-research/

Sweeney, E., & Dolgoff, S. (2024, February 23). *35 subtle gaslighting phrases that are unfairly belittling your emotions.* Good Housekeeping. https://www.goodhousekeeping.com/life/relationships/g39041313/gaslighting-phrases/

Taware, A. (2023, October 30). *The ethical tightrope: Navigating dark psychology in everyday life.* Medium. https://medium.com/@avtaware5/the-ethical-tightrope-navigating-dark-psychology-in-everyday-life-ba1e00957d66

Tripathi, Dr. A. (2023, April 6). *Definition and history of dark psychology.* Social Psychology. https://www.socialpsychology.info/dark-psychology/

Understanding dark psychology and manipulation in relationships. (2023, August 1). 2 Minutes Psychology. https://2minutespsychology.com/blog/understanding-dark-psychology-and-manipulation-in-relationships

Vettorello, M. (2021, February 4). *Anticipatory thinking: An essential 21st century skill*. Medium. https://medium.com/swlh/anticipatory-thinking-an-essential-21st-century-skill-4349cb656ce3

Vilhauer, J. (2019, September 29). *5 ways to keep yourself from being manipulated*. Psychology Today. https://www.psychologytoday.com/us/blog/living-forward/201909/5-ways-keep-yourself-being-manipulated

Vogel, K., & Craft, C. (2022, April 15). *How to spot manipulation tactics*. Psych Central. https://psychcentral.com/lib/tactics-manipulators-use-to-win-and-confuse-you

Waqas, A., Rehman, A., Malik, A., Muhammad, U., Khan, S., & Mahmood, N. (2015). Association of ego defense mechanisms with academic performance, anxiety and depression in medical students: A mixed methods study. *Cureus, 7*(9). https://doi.org/10.7759/cureus.337

Willis Benjamin Klein, Li, S., & Wood, S. (2023). A qualitative analysis of gaslighting in romantic relationships. *Personal Relationships, 30*(4). https://doi.org/10.1111/pere.12510

Word of the year 2022. (2023, November 26). Merriam-Webster. https://www.merriam-webster.com/wordplay/word-of-the-year-2022

54639304R00108